THE B-17
FLYING FORTRESS

ROBERT JACKSON

SPELLMOUNT
Staplehurst

British Library Cataloguing in Publication Data:
A catalogue record for this book is available
from the British Library

Copyright © Amber Books Ltd 2001

ISBN 1-86227-106-2

First published in the UK in 2001 by
Spellmount Limited
The Old Rectory
Staplehurst
Kent TN12 0AZ

Tel: 01580 893730
Fax: 01580 893731
Email: enquiries@spellmount.com
Website: www.spellmount.com

1 3 5 7 9 8 6 4 2

Editorial and design:
Amber Books Ltd
Bradley's Close, 74-77 White Lion Street,
London N1 9PF

Project Editor: Charles Catton
Editor: David Norman
Design: Nick Buzzard/Mark Batley
Picture Research: TRH Pictures

Printed and bound in the Slovak Republic

Picture credits
Boeing: 9, 10, 11, 16, 23, 30 (both), 82-83. Chrysalis Picture Library: 6-7, 13 (t), 17, 18-19, 27
(b), 90, 91. The Robert Hunt Library: 20, 36, 37, 41, 56 (IWM). TRH Pictures: 2-3, 8, 12, 14, 15,
21, 22, 27 (t), 28 (t) (Boeing), 32-33, 34, 42-43 (Smithsonian Institution), 44, 45 (t), 46, 47
(IWM), 48, 49, 50, 51 (both), 52-53, 56-57, 58-59, 60, 61 (IWM), 62 (IWM), 63, 66 (IWM), 67,
68, 69, 70 (t), 71, 72-73, 74 (t), 75, 76-77, 79, 80 (t), 84-85, 86, 87, 89.

Artwork credits
Aerospace Publishing Ltd: 28 (b), 35, 45 (b), 54-55, 70 (b), 74 (b), 78, 80 (b), 83, 88. Richard
Burgess: 38-39, 64-65. De Agostini UK: 13. Pilot Press: 24-25.

Pages 2-3: B-17G Flying Fortresses parked up on an East Anglian airfield in
the last year of World War II.

CONTENTS

CHAPTER 1

The Origins of the B-17 Flying Fortress

It seems strange that the seed of an idea that would one day develop into one of the world's finest strategic bombers, the Boeing B-17 Flying Fortress, should have been sown aboard an aircraft carrier, and yet that is how it happened.

In the spring of 1928 Clairmont J. Egtvedt, a vice-president of the Boeing Aircraft Company, boarded the carrier USS *Langley*, anchored in San Diego Bay, to confer with Rear-Admiral Joseph M. Reeves about the new Boeing F3B and F4B series of shipboard fighters, which were about to replace the earlier F2B in service with the US Navy. Importantly for Boeing's order book, the F4B had also been selected by the US Army Air Corps, which designated it the P-12 fighter.

Eventually, the conversation turned to a touchy subject. In 1920, a select committee known as the Cromwell Commission, having made a study of the recent air war in France, had recommended that a separate air force on a par with the Army and Navy should be established, just as Britain had done in April 1918 when the Royal Flying Corps and the Royal Naval Air Service had merged to become the Royal Air Force. The idea immediately provoked a hostile reaction from the US Navy, which saw its battleships as the nation's first line of defence, and considered the notion that the bomber might one day become the country's main offensive instrument to be preposterous.

On the other hand, a hard core of Army Air Corps officers had emerged from the war convinced that the future of America's military might lay with the long-range bomber. The staunchest advocate was Brigadier-General William Mitchell, who had commanded the flying units supporting the US First Army in France and who had embarked on what amounted to a crusade in his determination to prove the point. In the

Left: An Eighth Army Air Force B-17 formation heading for a target in Germany, silhouetted against a dense overcast sky. Unescorted daylight bomber formations were extremely vulnerable to fighter attack.

end, the Navy had agreed to participate in a series of trials, the aim being to prove (or disprove) that aircraft bombs were capable of sinking battleships.

In June 1921, a small fleet of captured German warships and time-expired American ones was assembled off the Virginia Capes, some 156km (97 miles) from where Mitchell's bombers were based at Langley Field. The trials began on 21 June, and on that day the German submarine *U117* was sunk by 12 bombs dropped from 335m (1100ft) by US Navy Curtiss F5L flying boats. On the 29th, Navy aircraft located the radio-controlled US battleship *Iowa* in 1 hour 57 minutes after being alerted of her approach somewhere within a 64,725 square kilometre (25,000 square mile) sea area and attacked her with dummy bombs; on 13 July the Army's Martin MB-2 bombers sank the German

destroyer *G-102*; and on 18 July the light cruiser *Frankfurt* went down under the combined effect of 74 bombs delivered by Army and Navy aircraft.

The real test came on 20 July, when Army, Navy and Marine Corps aircraft began a series of attacks on the 23,166-tonne (22,800-ton) German battleship *Ostfriesland*. She was a modern ship, only completed in 1912, and she was heavily compartmented. Her design reflected the German Navy's belief that it was much easier to repair a severely damaged battleship than to build another to replace one that had been sunk. On the first day the aircraft involved in the trial dropped 52 136kg (300lb) and 272kg (600lb) bombs on her, with no result, but on the following day she was sent to the bottom by 453kg (1000lb) and 906kg (2000lb) bombs that had been developed specifically for the task. In September

Above: The Boeing Monomail brought about a revolution in American commercial air transport. A clean design, it featured a number of innovations, including a retractable landing gear.

Left: A phosphorus bomb explodes over the discarded American battleship USS _Alabama_ during the bombing trials organised by Brigadier-General Billy Mitchell in September 1921.

the obsolete battleship USS _Alabama_ was also sunk by a direct hit from a single 906kg (2000lb) bomb.

The results of the tests were analysed by members of a joint Army–Navy Board under the chairmanship of General John J. Pershing. They seized on the fact that the air attacks on the warships had been unopposed, and that the bombers had consequently been able to carry them out from a very low level. The warships, moreover, had been stationary. The conclusion of the Board was that the battleship's position as the main bastion of America's sea defences would remain unchanged, although it recommended that aircraft carriers be developed as auxiliary vessels. The role of their aircraft would be to detect an enemy fleet and harass it until the defending battleships could close and engage it with their heavy armament.

As the naval aircraft then in service were armed with no more than four 104kg (230lb) bombs or one 226kg (500lb) bomb, they could hardly be expected to make serious dents in the enemy's armour. The board also conceded that land-based aircraft might also have a part to play in defending the coast against enemy attack.

Admiral Reeves fully supported the doctrine that confirmed the battleship as the supreme offensive and defensive weapon, and told Egtvedt so. No aircraft then flying could be remotely compared with the battleship.

BEGINNINGS OF THE B-17

Clairmont Egtvedt left the USS _Langley_ to fly back to Boeing's company base at Seattle with the germ of a challenge in his mind. He was certain that a bomber could be built that would outstrip the battleship in terms of offensive power; but how to design and build such an aircraft seemed to present insurmountable problems. Apart from anything else, the 1920s had seen the wholesale dismemberment of the war machine that had brought the Allies victory in 1918; the US Congress was adopting an increasingly isolationist stance, and was unlikely to vote funds for the development of aircraft (or engines to power them) that might or might not be needed in some future war. Besides, any such war would be no affair of America's; her only concern would be to defend her own integrity, and the capital ships of the United States Navy could ensure that. In fact Congress refused to budget any funds for the development of either military or civil aviation in the immediate post-war years.

Neither was there much incentive for aviation constructors to develop new aircraft as private ventures. After 1918 the market was flooded with thousands of surplus military machines, most of them in mint condition, crated and ready for shipment overseas, and they were sold off to anyone who wanted them at ridiculously cheap prices. Some enterprising businessmen, with an eye to the future, bought several aircraft and made determined attempts to found an airline. Some survived; most did not. One of the survivors was Boeing Air Transport, founded by Edward Hubbard.

As was also the case in Europe, the key to the development of civil aviation in the 1920s was the carriage of mail. In the USA, no fewer than seven committees sat between 1918 and 1924 to investigate the possibilities of using commercial aircraft as mail carriers; all of them had made favourable recommendations to Congress, which were ignored until 1925, when Congress passed the Air Mail Act, turning over the carriage of air mail to private contractors.

There was already a coast-to-coast air mail route, which was flown by military aircraft on charter to the US Post Office, but under the new Act bids were invited for certain connections to this route. The race was on, and to the competitors it was clear that the lucrative contract would go to those equipped with fast, long-range aircraft. Once again, there was incentive for development, and it was by this roundabout route that the B-17 would come into being.

Rising to the challenge of developing an effective mail-carrier, Clairmont Egtvedt and Edward Hubbard initiated the design of an all-metal commercial monoplane, with Charles N. Montieth as project engineer. The aircraft that emerged was the Boeing Model 200 Monomail, a very clean low-wing design featuring a retractable landing gear housed in a thick wing of cantilever construction. The aircraft was powered by a 570hp Pratt & Whitney Hornet radial engine, and first flew in May 1930. With all its features, the Model 200 could lay claim to being the first truly modern commercial aircraft.

NEW BOEING AIRCRAFT

The Model 200 Monomail was followed by the Model 221, with provision for six passengers in addition to cargo space between the engine and the pilot's open cockpit, which was situated well aft. The further refined Model 221A had space for eight passengers. With a wingspan of 18.03m (59ft 1in) and a length of 12.76m (41ft 10in) the Model 221A Monomail was a fairly large aircraft, weighing in at 3624kg (8000lb). It cruised at 217km/h (135mph), had a ceiling of 4480m (14,700ft) and a range of 925km (575 miles). It had the benefit of a three-bladed propeller, and its performance would undoubtedly have been enhanced had this been fitted with variable pitch; but in 1931, when the Model 221A made its appearance, this innovation was still in the future.

Meanwhile, Boeing had not neglected its interest in military projects. In January 1930, as a private venture, designer John Sanders began work on a bomber project using the Monomail design as his basis. The result was a twin-engined aircraft bearing the Company designation Model 215. The Air Corps encouraged the project, although no funds were made available, and the aircraft flew for the first time on 29 April

Below: The Boeing B-9 could outrun most pursuit aircraft of its day. Delays caused by technical problems, however, resulted in the Glenn Martin Company's B-10 winning the Air Corps' bomber contest.

Above: The Boeing Model 247 commercial airliner represented another big step forward in aircraft design. It brought Boeing within reach of its goal, the design of a successful long-range strategic bomber.

1931 with the military designation YB-9. An aerodynamically very clean low-wing monoplane, the YB-9 was powered by two Pratt & Whitney R-1831-13 engines producing 600hp at 1830m (6000ft). The YB9 prototype achieved a speed of 262 km/h (163mph). Testing revealed some problems, including excessive engine vibration and a tendency of the fuselage to twist in flight, and after various improvements, the now-named Y1B-9A's top speed was raised to 299km/h (186 mph), faster than any of its contemporaries and most fighter aircraft of the time. The aircraft's wingspan was 23.4m (76ft 10in), length was 15.7m (51ft 6in) and height 3.66m (12ft).

The production Boeing B-9 had a maximum range of 1593km (990 miles) with 526 gallons of fuel, and a combat radius of 434km (270 miles) with a 996kg (2200lb) bomb load. Rate of climb was 4.5m/sec (900ft/min), and operational ceiling 6862m (22,500ft).

The B-9 carried its bomb load in an internal bomb bay at the centre of gravity, but could carry additional bombs on external wing racks. The aircraft had a four-man crew; the bombardier/front gunner was installed in a nose cockpit that mounted a bomb sight in a sighting window in the floor, a flexible 0.30 calibre machine gun being mounted on a ring at the top of the cockpit, while the pilot and co-pilot sat in tandem cockpits because of the narrowness of the fuselage. The rear gunner sat in a cockpit aft of the wing trailing edge; all cockpits were open. The B-9 was the first American aircraft to feature servo tabs mounted on the movable control surfaces in order to assist the pilots to overcome increased loads at the top of the speed range.

Disappointingly for Boeing, the Air Corps ordered only six production B-9s, plus the prototype; the big defence contract went to the Glenn L. Martin Company's B-10 bomber, which was to be the backbone of the Air Corps' bomber arm for the next decade to come. Nevertheless, Boeing quickly bounced back with another commercial design, based on the B-9 bomber. This was the Model 247, an aircraft that was to revolutionise air transport.

The Boeing 247 prototype, which was designed to carry ten passengers and a crew consisting of pilot, co-pilot and stewardess, made its maiden flight on 8 February 1933, and immediately made the entire world of commercial aircraft seem obsolete. Like its B-9 precursor, the new aircraft had an all-metal structure and was a low-wing monoplane with a retractable undercarriage. It was very streamlined, had good all-round performance and low operating costs, and its technical innovations included a wing and tail de-icing system. United Air Lines had a complete monopoly of the 247 production line, having invested the then fantastic sum of $3 million in an order for 60 aircraft before the prototype had even flown, and Boeing Air Transport, which was part of the United Group, introduced the first 247 into service on 30 March 1933.

Not only did the 247 cut eight hours off the trans-continental service; it also combined speed with a high standard of comfort. In its first month of service, it brought United a massive increase in ticket sales. Then, on 10 October 1933, a 247 bound for Chicago exploded in mid-air over Indiana, killing all seven on board. The aircraft was not at fault – the disaster had been caused by an explosive item of cargo that

Below: The Boeing Model 299, prototype of the Flying Fortress, is rolled out at Seattle on 17 July 1935. The aircraft's elegance and impression of power caused a media sensation.

had found its way on board – but the aircraft inevitably lost some of its passenger appeal as a result. Nevertheless, its future might have been assured if Boeing had been in a position to sell it to TransWorld Airlines, which wanted it badly; but at that time Boeing and United were both still controlled by the same board of directors, and they turned down the competing TWA's application.

DOUGLAS DC-1

Jack Frye, TWA's president, turned to another manufacturer: Donald Douglas. The result was the DC-1, precursor of the DC2, the first of which was delivered to TWA on 14 May 1934. The DC-2 carried four more passengers than the Boeing 247 and was 40km/h (25mph) faster; suddenly, the day of the 247 was over. From now on, although Boeing's name would become a synonym for long-range air transport, it would be Douglas machines that would dominate the domestic routes of the United States, and of half the world. However the short-lived Model 247 left a lasting legacy. It was the final link in the chain that led directly to Clairmont Egtvedt's 'flying battleship'.

In 1934, in response to a rapidly worsening international situation – Japan had invaded Manchuria in the previous year

and had left the League of Nations, followed by Nazi Germany, effectively destroying any hope of disarmament – the US Army Air Corps, following feasibility studies by the Material Division at Wright Field, initiated 'Project A', which called for the building of a bomber capable of carrying a payload of one ton over a distance of 8045km (5000 miles); in other words, an aircraft that could fly non-stop to American bases in Panama, Hawaii and Alaska from the continental USA. The General Staff gave its approval for the development of such an aircraft, and on 12 May 1934 negotiations began with Boeing and Martin for preliminary designs and engineering data. In June, Boeing was awarded a preliminary contract for the construction of a single aircraft under the designation XBLR-1 (Experimental Bomber, Long Range Model 1) abbreviated later to XB-15. It was to be the largest aircraft ever built in the United States, with a wingspan of 45.5m (149ft) and a length of 26.7m (87ft 7in).

Work on the XB-15 design had scarcely begun when, on 8 August 1934, the Boeing Engineering Department received a

Above: The end of Model 299 at Wright Field, Ohio, on October 30 1935. The crash was caused by human error, one of the crew having omitted to release the device that locked the elevators.

circular from Wright Field. It contained specifications for a new production bomber (as distinct from the experimental XB-15) to replace the Martin B-10 currently in service. The requirement envisaged a multi-engined aircraft capable of carrying a ton of bombs at more than 322km/h (200mph) over a range of 3218km (2000 miles). The company that sub-

Below: The cockpit of the Flying Fortress. Its layout varied as successive B-17 models were produced, but only slightly. In fact, the whole B-17 design underwent very little change throughout its service life.

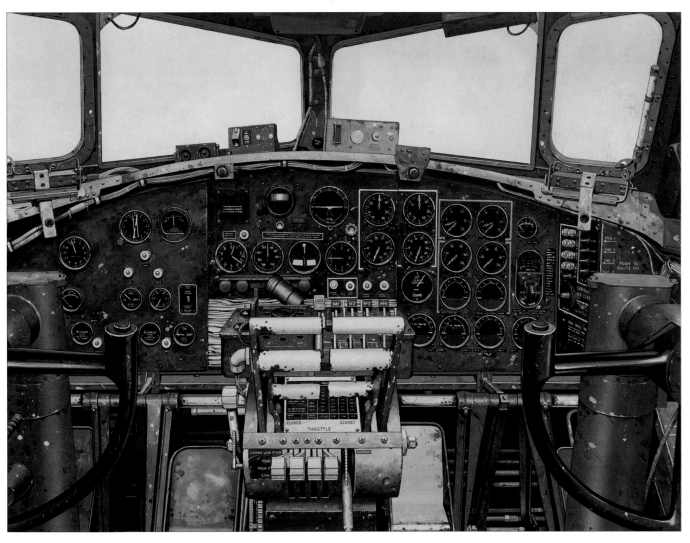

mitted the successful tender would be assured of an order for as many as 220 aircraft. The prototype was to be ready to fly within a year.

THE MODEL 299

Boeing's response was the Model 299. Project engineer was E.G. Emery, with Edward C. Wells as his assistant. Wells had worked on the design of the Model 247's tail section; before 1935 was out he would have taken over from Emery as project engineer. He was just 24 years old.

Because of the low power of existing aero-engines, Boeing decided to make the Model 299 a four-engine design. The Company invested $275,000 of its own capital in the design and construction of the new aircraft, and with all its facilities devoted to the task the prototype bomber was ready to be rolled out on 17 July 1935. The maiden flight followed on 28 July, with Boeing's Chief Test Pilot Leslie R. Tower at the controls; he reported that the big aircraft's performance was even more outstanding than had been expected. In fact, the Model 299 was a shining example of the aircraft designer's

adage that if an aircraft looks good, it will fly well; and the 299 was certainly a handsome beast.

Boeing knew it had a winner; it remained only to convince the Army Air Corps. At 0342 on 20 August 1935, Leslie Tower lifted the Model 299 off Seattle's runway at the start of a demonstration flight. With him he carried Louis Wait as co-pilot, with C.W. Benton of Boeing and Henry Igo of Pratt & Whitney as observers. Nine hours later, the 299 touched down at Wright Field near Dayton, Ohio, having made a non-stop flight of 3379km (2100 miles) at an average speed of 373km/h (232mph), using only 63 per cent of the available 3000hp. The flight was made at an average altitude of 3812m (12,500ft), mostly on autopilot. Tower and his crew were met at Wright Field by Egtvedt and Wells, and were delighted to learn they had made such good time that the Air Corps officials were not expecting them for another two hours.

Below: A B-17 starts her engines on a test while ground crew wait with fire extinguishers at the ready. All B-17 variants (except the Model 299) used the same Wright 1820 radial engines.

The Boeing 299 was to be evaluated against two other contenders, the Martin 146 and Douglas DB-1, both of which were twin-engined types. The Air Corps assigned Lt Donald Putt to the Model 299 as project test pilot, and in the series of preliminary test flights that followed he reported that the aircraft exceeded all Army specifications for speed, rate of climb, range and payload capability.

The final evaluation flights were to be made under the jurisdiction of Major Ployer P. Hill, head of Wright Field's Testing Section, and it was Hill who was in the left-hand pilot's seat as aircraft captain when the 299 taxied out on 30 October 1935. Donald Putt was in the co-pilot's seat, with Tower standing behind and Igo and Benton further aft.

The Model 299 gathered speed along the runway, lifted off, began to climb – then stalled, turned on one wing and plunged to the ground, bursting into flames upon impact. By the time rescuers arrived at the scene Putt, Igo and Benton had managed to stagger from the blazing wreck, but Hill and Tower were still trapped inside. With great gallantry, First Lieutenant Robert K. Giovannoli risked his life to pull first Tower and then Hill from the shattered cockpit (an act for which he was given the Cheney Award, only to die in a later air crash before he could receive it). Hill never regained consciousness and died later in the afternoon; Tower lingered on for a few more days, but then he died of his injuries. The others survived, although all were badly burned, as was Giovannoli himself.

HUMAN ERROR

Luckily for the aircraft's future prospects, an investigation soon revealed that the crash had been caused by human, rather than mechanical error. To prevent damage to the tail surfaces when the aircraft was parked in a strong wind, the aircraft was fitted with a device that locked the elevators in position. This device was released by levers in the cockpit, a procedure that formed part of the pre-flight checks, but on this occasion this vital action had not been carried out. Tower had tried to reach the levers at the last moment, but had been too late to prevent disaster.

Before the accident, the Air Corps had recommended the initial purchase of 65 B-17s, as the bomber was to be designated in service, but in January 1937 the General Staff was willing to authorise a production contract for only 13 pre-production machines under the designation Y1B-17, along with 133 twin-engined Douglas B-18 medium bombers. The Y1B-17 design differed from the Model 299 only in its engines, the Pratt & Whitneys having been replaced by more powerful 850hp Wright 1820s, and in a minor modification to the undercarriage.

The first Y1B-17 (serial 36-149) was delivered to the 2nd Bombardment Group at Langley Field on 1 March 1937, and the twelfth machine arrived on 5 August that year. The thirteenth aircraft was assigned to the Materiel Division at Wright Field for test purposes, while a fourteenth aircraft

Above: An early model B-17 runs up its engines prior to takeoff from Wright Field. The redesign of the tail unit from the B-17E onwards made it possible to install a more effective tail gun position.

was earmarked to be tested to destruction on the ground. In fact, this never happened, thanks to what turned out to be a lucky accident when a 2nd BG aircraft, fully loaded and instrumented, encountered severe turbulence in a storm over Langley Field and went into a spin. The pilot recovered and made a safe landing; when the aircraft was inspected it was found to be repairable, even though the wings were bent, rivets popped, and the test instruments showed that it had exceeded all maximum permissible G loadings. The fourteenth aircraft was consequently fitted with turbo-superchargers for high-altitude experimental flying and retained at Wright Field under the designation Y1B-17A. This sole example, serialled 37369, differed from the others in that it was fitted with Wright R1850-21 engines and General Electric superchargers.

The 2nd was now the USAAC's sole heavy bombardment group, and the task of ushering the Y1B-17 into full service fell to the Group Commander, Lt Col Robert C. Olds. During the months that followed, the 2nd Bombardment Group's hand-picked crews were to log 9293 flying hours over land and sea, in all weathers, covering a total distance of 2,896,200km (1,800,000 miles) the equivalent of 72 circuits of the earth at the equator – without serious mishap.

In the process they established a number of noteworthy records. At the beginning of 1938 a Y1B-17 captained by Lt Col Olds crossed the United States from east to west in 12 hours 50 minutes, then made the return crossing in 10 hours 46 minutes at an average speed of 394km/h (245mph). This was followed, on 15 February, by a flight from Langley to Buenos Aires, Argentina, the six aircraft involved refuelling in Miami before setting out on the longest leg of the flight to Lima, Peru. This 4336km (2695-mile) stretch was completed without incident in 15 hours and 32 minutes, and flight time for the leg from Lima to Buenos Aires, of 3216km

(2000 miles), was 11 hours 5 minutes, the aircraft having climbed to 6405m (21,000ft) to cross the Andes.

The six bombers arrived back at Langley on 27 February 1938, and the 2nd Bombardment Group's record-breaking flight – the longest up to that date – brought the unit the award of the Mackay Trophy. The aircraft commanders involved were Lt Col Olds, Major Vincent J. Meloy, Captain Neil B. Harding, Major Caleb V. Haynes, Captain Archibald Y. Smith, and Major Harold George, all of whom were to make notable contributions during World War II. So would some of their crew members; they included a young pilot (acting as navigator on this occasion) called Curtis Emerson LeMay, who would later lead the strategic air offensive against Japan and go on post-war to command Strategic Air Command, the most powerful and perhaps numerous air strike force the world would ever see.

Above: The Boeing XB-15 was the first of America's very heavy bomber designs. The huge 35-ton aircraft flew for the first time in October 1937 and was used as a transport in World War II.

While the 2nd Bombardment Group was making powerful demonstrations of the heavy bomber's potential, however, equally powerful forces were at work which threatened to strangle the concept before it could be fully realised. In May 1938 Louis A. Johnson, the Assistant Secretary of War, received a memo from the Adjutant General stating that military aircraft development during the fiscal years 1939-40 would be restricted to fighters and close-support machines. No funding would be available for the development of four-engined heavy bombers. It was a serious blow to Boeing, which had used its own funds to build the Model 299 in anticipation of large orders for the production aircraft.

Instead, in the summer of 1938 there were only the 13 Y1B-17s, one Y1B-17A, and an order for 39 production B-17Bs.

The US Navy was also keen to plunge its knife into the corpse of the heavy bomber, an ambition that was unintentionally damaged by the GHQ Air Corps when it sent three aircraft of the 2nd Bombardment Group on a search mission to locate the Italian liner *Rex*, inbound for New York. With Lt Col Olds in the lead and Lt LeMay navigating, the liner was duly sighted at a distance of 1126km (700 miles) from the US east coast, amply vindicating the theory that the bomber could intercept and attack an enemy fleet at long range.

NAVY PROTEST

The Navy lodged a protest with the General Staff, maintaining that it was its task, and its task alone, to counter any seaborne threat at a distance of more than 160km (100 miles) from the American coast. The upshot was that the War Department issued a verbal order limiting all Army Air Corps activities to the sea area within the 160km (100-mile) demarcation line, effectively denying the 2nd BG's crews the opportunity to train for long-range flights over water and make recommendations on how best to conduct them.

During the celebrations to mark the 30th anniversary of the US Army Air Corps, held in July and August 1939, the B-17s went on to break several more national and international speed, payload and altitude records. By this time the 2nd Bombardment Group had completed its trials, the 'Y'

Below: Boeing B-17Cs awaiting delivery to the Royal Air Force, before Pearl Harbor. The RAF never used the Fortress I properly in the bomber role, and it was quickly withdrawn after suffering losses.

having been dropped from the bomber's designation, and one of the records was established by the first production B-17B, which flew from Seattle to New York in nine hours and 14 minutes at an average speed of 426km/h (265mph).

The Boeing XB-15 also took part in these events. The massive, 35-ton aircraft had flown for the first time in October 1937, and although it was underpowered and unable to reach its designed maximum speed, it had a long range and was capable of lifting considerable payloads. Early in 1939 it had made the headlines by flying a mercy mission to Chile, carrying a load of food and medical supplies to the aid of earthquake victims, and on 8 August 1939 it established a new payload-to-altitude record by lifting 15,000kg (33,000lb) to 2501m (8200ft). The XB-15 went on to see service in World War II in the transport role as the XC-105.

In addition to the order for 30 B-17Bs, Boeing had now received a second order for 39 B-17Cs, and a further order for the B-17D variant was being negotiated. Behind the scenes acrimonious discussions were in progress between the company and the Air Corps over the unit cost per aircraft. According to the original contracts a unit price of $205,000 had been agreed, but the Air Corps now insisted that this was too high. The whole B-17 programme hung in the balance, even when Boeing advised the War Department that it could get its rock-bottom price down to $202,500 by deleting some features such as the external bomb racks. In the end an agreement was reached, and the heavy bomber programme was saved. The agreement came only just in time, for the writing was on the wall for America's isolationist policies. On 1 September 1939, Hitler's armies smashed into Poland, and plunged the world into war.

CHAPTER 2

The Evolution of the B-17

From the very beginning of the design process, the B-17 was intended to be an aircraft with a rugged strength and great endurance, yet easy to manufacture in large numbers. The resulting design was a classic of its time, able to absorb changes and upgrades, particularly to its defensive armament, without the need to make substantial alterations to its airframe.

Strength was a key factor in the design of the B-17. Uppermost in the minds of its designers was the knowledge that they not only had to produce an aircraft required to carry a substantial bomb load over great distances, but also one capable of sustaining considerable punishment from enemy defences, and still surviving. Moreover, the aircraft had to be tailored to mass production, so the basic design had to be subjected to as few changes as possible as it evolved. In other words, the designers had to get it right first time; and the proof that they did lies in the fact that although the B-17 underwent thousands of modifications during its lifetime, the basic design was never altered.

In designing the fuselage, Edward C. Wells – who had chosen that particular part of the aircraft as his personal project – selected a circular cross-section, partly because it had an efficient strength-to-weight ratio and partly for ease of construction. The fuselage was an all-metal, semi-monocoque structure with a maximum depth of 2.6m (8.6ft) and a width of 2.3m (7.5ft); structural strength was evenly distributed throughout its length, so that damage to important structural members of the airframe would not result in catastrophic failure.

All the way through in the early models, and as far back as the tail gunner's compartment from the B-17E model onwards, the fuselage was constructed of bulkheads and circumferential stiffeners joined by longerons and longitudinal stiffeners. The framework was covered with a skin of

Left: Ground crew at work on a B-17. This photograph gives a good idea of the bomber's size. The B-17 carried three main fuel tanks in the inboard sections of each wing, and nine in the outboard sections.

24ST Alclad, fastened with aluminium rivets; the thickness of the skin varied, being heavier at loadbearing sections.

To assist mass production the fuselage was built in four sections, all of which were assembled on jigs and brought together into one piece on the production line. The forward section, containing the positions for the two pilots and the navigator-bombardier, extended from the nose to the bulkhead immediately aft of the cockpit; the centre section housed the bomb bay; and finally came the rear fuselage and tail sections.

The wing centre section was incorporated in the fuselage, and like the fuselage the wing was of semi-monocoque structure, using two main spars of truss (bridge-like) design. The aerofoil section combined the NACA 0018 at the wing root with 0010 at the tip; chord at the wing root was 579cm (228in), and wing area was 131.9m² (1420 sq ft).

The wing was constructed in six sections, right and left inboard, right and left outboard, and the tips. The inboard sections housed the engines, flaps and landing gear, while the ailerons were fitted into the outer sections. The two main spars were of truss-type construction, the trusses being aluminium tubes riveted together to form a single unit, and the spars were joined together by ribs spaced 38 to 46cm (15 to 18in) apart. The wing was covered with Alclad sheet aluminium with the exception of the control surfaces, which were fabric covered. The left aileron was fitted with a trim tab. De-icer strips were installed in the leading edges of the outer wing panels and between the engines. The split-type flaps were electrically operated, but could so be raised and lowered manually if necessary.

ENGINES AND UNDERCARRIAGE

The engine nacelles were connected to the inboard wing sections by bulkheads at the front spar. The inboard nacelles housed the landing gear, which retracted into strongly reinforced wheel wells. Both main wheels and tail wheel were electrically operated, but the main wheels could be raised and lowered manually in an emergency. The inboard wing sections also housed the three main fuel tanks and there were nine more in the outer sections, giving a total fuel overload capacity of 10,522 litres (2780 US gallons). With the addition of bomb bay tanks, the fuel uplift could be increased to 13,626 litres (3600 US gallons). All fuel tanks were self-sealing from the B-17E model onwards. (The RAF insisted on its B-17C Fortress Is being fitted with self-sealing tanks before these aircraft were delivered).

Left: B-17s on the production line at Seattle. The B-17 was optimised for mass production; the B-17F and B-17G variants were also built by the Douglas Aircraft Corporation and Lockheed Vega.

Right: The chin turret position on a B-17G. The chin turret was first introduced in the B-17F and was developed in response to head-on attacks by German fighters, which had become common by late 1943.

The B-17 Flying Fortress was a robust yet aesthetically pleasing aircraft with no inherent vices. But it was a war machine, and to help it perform its task it had the benefit of a very sophisticated item of equipment: the Norden bombsight. Very accurate and highly secret, the sight was developed by Carl L. Norden and Captain Frederick I. Entwistle, assistant research chief of the Navy Bureau of Ordnance.

The main component of the Norden's sighting head was a gyroscopically-stablised, motor-driven telescope, through which the bombardier viewed the target during the attack run. Having fed the appropriate windspeed and altitude calculations into the sight, together with the bombs' ballistic data, the bombardier then held the target centred in the telescope's sighting graticule. Precise information on the bomber's movement over the ground was fed into the Norden's sighting computer, enabling the bombardier to control lateral movements of the aircraft through the Automatic Flight Control Equipment (AFCE, popularly called the Autopilot). As long as the sight was pointed at the target, the aircraft remained under automatic control until

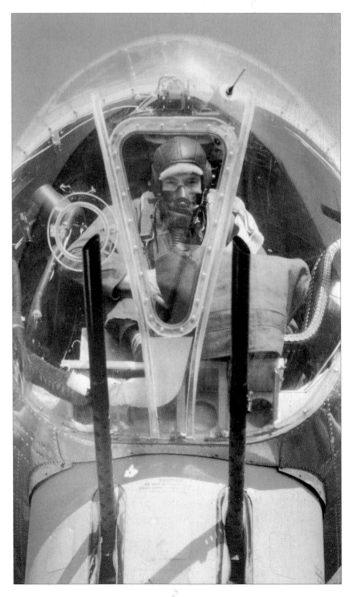

the bombs were released, which was also an automatic process, the ballistic angle being calculated by the sight's computer. With the bombs away, the bombardier would cut out the sight and restore command of the aircraft to the pilot. In clear conditions, devastatingly precise bombing results could be achieved with the Norden; but when the B-17 went to war, it would be in skies over Europe and the Mediterranean that were usually anything but clear.

The early model B-17s (B-17B to B-17D) were, in common with other American bomber types of the period, designed for a defensive rather than an offensive role: in other words, their primary function in time of war would be to attack an enemy invasion force threatening the continental United States itself. It was not anticipated that they would come under heavy enemy fighter attack while carrying out this task. This thinking was reflected in the choice of armament for the early operational models; up to and including the B-17D, this did not exceed seven machine guns of mixed calibre (0.30 and 0.50in), most of them on flexible mountings and hand-held.

THE NOSE TURRET

The early B-17 variants had a single hand-held flexible 0.30in nose gun that could be fired by either the bombardier or the navigator. This wholly inadequate weapon was replaced by two 0.50in guns, one mounted on either side of the nose in the B-17F, but hand-held weapons of this kind had a poor degree of accuracy and their field of fire was limited. The last 86 B-17Fs were consequently fitted with a chin-mounted power-operated Bendix turret mounting a pair of 0.50in guns, which proved invaluable as the Luftwaffe increasingly adopted frontal fighter attacks. This became standard on the B-17G model, which mounted 13 0.50 calibre guns, forcing the Germans to add extra armour to their fighters.

Below: This photograph clearly illustrates the cramped conditions that had to be endured by the B-17's ball turret gunner. Normally, he could not wear a parachute while at his station.

Right: The dorsal gun position in an early-model B-17, showing the single flexibly-mounted gun. This was later replaced by a power-operated Bendix or Sperry turret with twin 0.5in machine guns.

Boeing B-17F Flying Fortress

1. Rudder construction
2. Rudder tab
3. Rudder tab actuation
4. Tail gunner's station
5. Gunsight
6. Twin 0.5in (12.7mm) machine guns
7. Tail cone
8. Tail gunner's seat
9. Ammunition troughs
10. Elevator trim tab
11. Starboard elevator
12. Tailplane structure
13. Tailplane front spar
14. Tailplane/fuselage attatchement
15. Control cables
16. Elevator control mechanism
17. Rudder control linkage

68. Bomb-bay central catwalk
69. Vertical bomb stowage racks (starbord installation shown)
70. Horizontal bomb stowage (port side shown)
71. Dinghy stowage
72. Twin 0.5in (12.7mm) machine guns
73. Dorsal turret
74. Port wing flaps
75. Cooling air slots

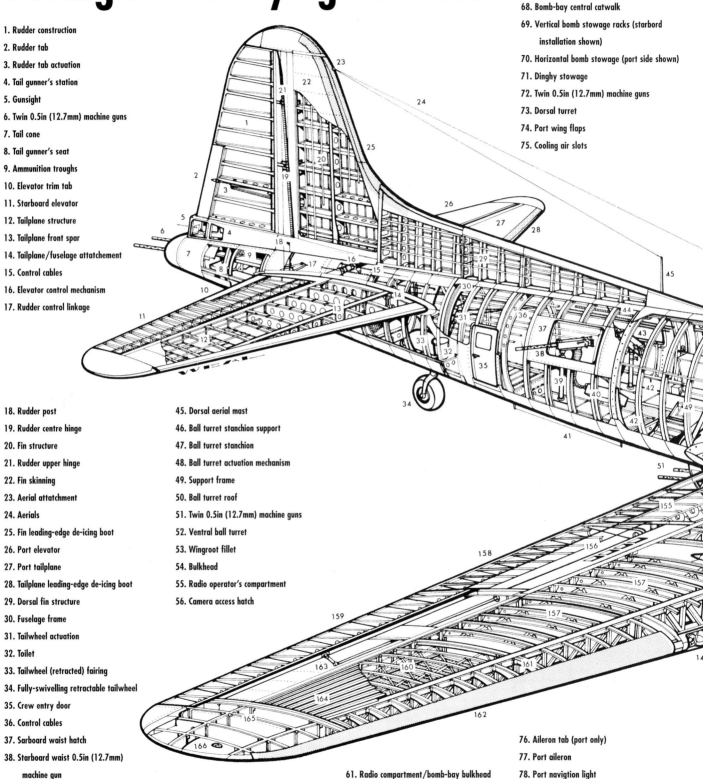

18. Rudder post
19. Rudder centre hinge
20. Fin structure
21. Rudder upper hinge
22. Fin skinning
23. Aerial attatchment
24. Aerials
25. Fin leading-edge de-icing boot
26. Port elevator
27. Port tailplane
28. Tailplane leading-edge de-icing boot
29. Dorsal fin structure
30. Fuselage frame
31. Tailwheel actuation
32. Toilet
33. Tailwheel (retracted) fairing
34. Fully-swivelling retractable tailwheel
35. Crew entry door
36. Control cables
37. Sarboard waist hatch
38. Starboard waist 0.5in (12.7mm) machine gun
39. Gun support frame
40. Ammunition box
41. Ventral aerial
42. Waist gunners' positions
43. Port waist 0.5in (12.7mm) machine gun
44. Ceiling control cable runs

45. Dorsal aerial mast
46. Ball turret stanchion support
47. Ball turret stanchion
48. Ball turret actuation mechanism
49. Support frame
50. Ball turret roof
51. Twin 0.5in (12.7mm) machine guns
52. Ventral ball turret
53. Wingroot fillet
54. Bulkhead
55. Radio operator's compartment
56. Camera access hatch

57. Radio compartment windows (port and starboard)
58. Ammuniton boxes
59. Single 0.3in (7.62mm) dorsal machine gun
60. Radio compartment roof glazing

61. Radio compartment/bomb-bay bulkhead
62. Fire extinguisher
63. Radio operator's station (port side)
64. Handrail links
65. Bulkead step
66. Wing rear spar/fuselage attatchment
67. Wingroot profile

76. Aileron tab (port only)
77. Port aileron
78. Port navigtion light
79. Wing skinning
80. Wing leading-edge de-icing boot
81. Port landing light
82. Wing corrugated inner skin
83. Port out wing fuel tank (nine inner rib cells)
84. No.1 engine nacelle

85. Cooling gills
86. Three-blade propellers
87. No.2 engine nacelle
88. Wing leading-edge de-icing boot
89. Port mid-wing (self sealing) fuel tanks
90. Flight deck upper glazing
91. Flight deck/bomb-bay bulkhead
92. Oxygen cylinders
93. Co-pilot's seat
94. Co-pilot's control column
95. Headrest/armour
96. Compass installation
97. Pilot's seat
98. Windscreen
99. Central control console pedestal
100. Side windows
101. Navigator's equipment

105. Enlarged cheek windows (flush)
106. Ammunition box
107. Bombardier's panel
108. Norden bombsight installation
109. Plexiglass frameless nose cone
110. Single 0.5in (12.7mm) nose machine gun
111. Optically-flat bomb-aiming panel
112. Pitot head fairing (port and starboard)
113. D/F loop bullet fairing
114. Port mainwheel
115. Flight deck underfloor control linkage
116. Wingroot/fuselage fairing
117. Wing front spar/fuselage attatchment
118. Battery access panels (wingroot
      leading-edge)
119. No.3 engine nacelle spar bulkhead

125. Retracted mainwheel (semi-recessed)
126. Firewall
127. Cooling gills
128. Exhaust collector ring assembly
129. Three-blade propellers
130. Undercarriage retraction struts
131. Starboard mainwheel
132. Axle
133. Mainwheel oleo leg
134. Propeller reduction gear casing
135. 1000hp Wright R-1829-65 radial engine

149. No.4 engine nacelle spar bulkhead
150. Oil radiator intake
151. Main spar web structure
152. Mid-wing fuel tank rib cut-outs
153. Auxillery mid spar
154. Rear spar
155. Landing flap profile
156. Cooling air slots

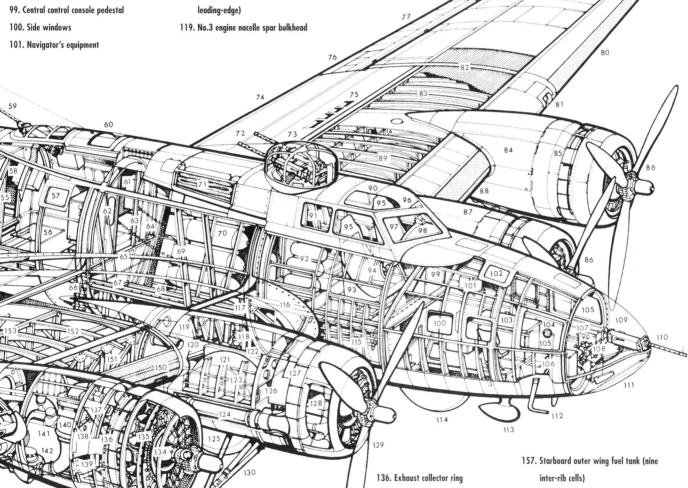

136. Exhaust collector ring
137. Engine upper bearers
138. Firewall
139. Engine lower bearers
140. Intercooler assembly
141. Oil tank (nacelle outboard wall)
142. Supercharger
143. Intake
144. Supercharger waste gear
145. Starboard landing light
146. Supercharger intake
147. Intercooler intake
148. Ducting

102. Navigator's compartment upper window
     (subsequently replaced by ceiling
     astrodome)
103. Navigator's table
104. Side gun mounting

120. Intercooler pressure duct
121. Mainwheel well
122. Oil tank (nacelle inboard wall)
123. Nacelle structure
124. Exhaust

157. Starboard outer wing fuel tank (nine
     inter-rib cells)
158. Flap structure
159. Starboard aileron
160. Outboard wing ribs
161. Spar assembly
162. Wing leading-edge de-icing boot
163. Aileron control linkage
164. Wing corrugated inner skin
165. Wingtip structure
166. Starboard navigation light

THE B-17'S LINEAGE AT A GLANCE

The B-17 Flying Fortress was designed in response to a USAAC competition in 1934, the prototype, powered by four 750hp Pratt & Whitney Hornet engines, flying on 28 July 1935. Thirteen Y1B-17s and one Y1B-17A were ordered for evaluation, and after the trial period these were designated B-17 and B-17A respectively. The first production batch of 39 B-17Bs, featuring a modified nose, enlarged rudder and various other modifications, were all delivered by the end of March 1940; meanwhile a further order had been placed for 38 B-17Cs, which were powered by four 1200hp Cyclone engines and featured some minor changes. Twenty of these were supplied to the RAF as the Fortress I in 1941, but after sustaining several losses on bombing operations the remainder were diverted to Coastal Command or the Middle East. By the time the Pacific war began the B-17D, 42 of which had been ordered in 1940, was in service. This was generally similar to the C model, and the Cs in service were subsequently modified to D standard.

The new tail design, the main recognition feature of all subsequent Fortresses, was introduced with the B-17E, together with improved armament which for the first time included a tail gun position. The RAF received 42 B-17Es in 1942 under the designation Fortress IIA; one B-17E was converted as the 38-passenger XC-108 transport for General Douglas MacArthur, C-in-C Pacific Theatre, another as the XC-108A freighter, and one, the XB-38, was experimentally fitted with Allison engines. The further refined B-17F entered production in April 1942, 61 examples of this variant being converted for reconnaissance as the F-9. Another 19 were delivered to RAF Coastal Command as the Fortress II.

The last production Fortress was the B-17G, featuring a 'chin' turret mounting two 0.50in guns. The RAF received 85 B-17Gs as the Fortress III. Ten B-17Gs were converted for reconnaissance as the F-9C, while the US Navy and Coast Guard used 24 PB-1Ws and 16 PB-1Gs for maritime surveillance and aerial survey. About 130 were modified for air-sea rescue duties as the B-17H or TB-17H, with a lifeboat carried under the fuselage and other rescue equipment. Production of the Fortress, from the B-17F onwards, was shared between Boeing, Douglas and Lockheed-Vega.

THE DORSAL TURRET

Like the nose turret, the dorsal gun position – a very important defensive position – featured only a single 0.30in machine gun in early model B-17s, mounted in a blister. This was soon replaced by either a power-operated Bendix or Sperry turret. The turret was well protected from the gunner's point of view, as he had substantial armour plate at his back and his head was protected by the breeches of the two 0.50in guns, one on either side. The main drawback was that the guns could only be elevated to an angle of 45 degrees, leaving a blind spot directly overhead.

THE VENTRAL TURRET

Early B-17 models had a 'bathtub'-type ventral gun position with a single 0.30in gun. This was replaced by a remotely operated Bendix turret whose guns were sighted by means of a periscope; this did not prove successful, and so it was replaced by a Sperry ball turret capable of rotating through the full 360 degrees on the horizontal plane and 90 degrees through the vertical plane. The ball turret was not a comfortable position; it had to be entered and abandoned during flight after it was rotated into the correct position, and a parachute could not normally be worn. The B-17 could not be belly-landed with the turret in the down position, and several gunners were killed when battle damage prevented the ball turret from being retracted, or from being rotated to allow the occupant to escape.

THE WAIST GUNS

Early Fortresses had waist gun blisters, which were deleted in later models and replaced by simple open windows. The flexible hand-held machine guns had a shock absorber incorporated in the gun mount to absorb recoil and vibrations. Whereas the turret-mounted guns had fire control cut-off cams, the waist guns had no such refinement. It was by no means unusual for a waist gunner to shoot pieces off his own aircraft in the excitement of tracking an enemy fighter. Although the waist gunners wore electrically-heated flying suits, their position was the most uncomfortable in the B-17. Until the introduction of glazed windows in the waist positions of the B-17G, hurricane-force winds often lashed the inside of the fuselage and temperatures could fall as low as 40 degrees below zero.

THE TAIL POSITION

The early model B-17Cs and Ds had no tail gun position. The B-17E was the first Fortress variant to be fitted with what was called a 'tail stinger' comprising twin 0.50in guns, and while these were manually operated and had a limited field of fire, they were far better than nothing at all. The original ring and bead sight eventually gave way to a reflector type, and then to a 'compensating' gunsight which required the gunner to know the dimensions of an attacking fighter so that the information could be fed into the sight to give accurate range.

Late B-17Gs had the Cheyenne gun turret, in which a canvas covering was replaced by a flush-fitting metal one with vertical slits for the guns to traverse in. B-17 tail gunners had no rear armour protection, and when German fighters adopted frontal attack tactics many of these crewmen lost their lives when bullets or shells penetrated the nose and passed down the full length of the fuselage interior to hit them in the back.

EXTRA FIREPOWER

Two single hand-operated 0.5in guns could be fired from socket-like flexible mounts in the Plexiglas nose or from small windows on either side of the fuselage; these were designed for use by the bombardier and navigator, adding to the B-17's defensive firepower when the bomber came under fighter attack.

Long before America's entry into the war, Edward C. Wells and the Boeing design team had begun modifying the basic

Right: The B-17 waist gunners had a difficult task, having to aim their hand-held weapons in an aircraft that was often taking evasive action. They even sometimes shot pieces off their own aircraft.

Below: Impressive shot of a B-17 running up its engines at night. The Fortress was designed as a daylight bomber and, except in the case of some special duties units, did not operate under cover of darkness.

B-17 to provide the aircraft with a greater offensive capability. The first move was to restructure the tail surfaces in order to give the bomber greater stability at high altitude, an important consideration when bombing precision targets.

From the B-17E onward, therefore, the Fortress was endowed with a large, sweeping dorsal fin to which a long fairing was added, substantially increasing the area of the vertical tail surfaces on the aircraft. The span of the tailplane (horizontal stabliser) was also increased by three metres (ten feet) to 13m (43ft). In addition, the rear fuselage of the B-17E was 1.8m (6ft) longer than that of the D model to permit the installation of twin 0.5in machine guns in the tail. As the B-17 became endowed with greater offensive capability, however, it was called upon to make deep penetration missions into enemy territory, and in the face of a

Below: Boeing B-17F-70-BO of the 322nd Bomb Squadron, 91st Bomb Group. The Eighth AAF adopted RAF-style three-letter identification code markings in 1943, but not all units employed them.

Above: A massive crowd greets the rollout of the 5000th B-17. More than 12,000 Flying Fortresses were produced, and some continued to serve in various roles long after the end of WWII.

hostile fighter environment its defensive armour and weaponry had to be increased, with a consequent weight penalty; the range and service ceiling of the B-17G were both less than those of its predecessor, the B-17F.

With an empty weight of 15,075kg (33,279lb), the B-17E was seven tons heavier than the original Model 299; it was also a good deal faster – 40 per cent faster, in fact – having a top speed of 512km/h (318mph). The B-17E was the first of what might be described as the 'offensive' Fortresses, intended for the primary role of strategic bombing.

Apart from a more elongated Plexiglas nose, designed to give the bombardier more working space and to improve his field of vision, and the provision of broad Hamilton Standard 'paddle'-type propellers designed to increase the operational ceiling, the next Fortress variant, the B-17F, was

THE B-17 VARIANTS - TECHNICAL DATA

MODEL 299
Span: 31.12m (103ft 9in).
Length: 20.96m (68ft 9in).
Weight empty: 9810kg (21,657lb).
All-up weight: 14,691kg (32,432lb).
Maximum speed: 379km/h (236mph) at 7625m (25,000ft).
Maximum range: 4843km (3010 miles) at 225km/h (140mph).
Service ceiling: 7509m (24,620ft).
Engines: Four 750hp Pratt & Whitney R-1690 radials.
Armament: Five 0.50 or 0.30in machine guns.
Maximum bomb load: 3624kg (8000lb).
Average bomb load: 1812kg (4000lb).

Y1B-17 (BOEING MODEL 299B)
Span: 31.12m (103ft 9in).
Length: 20.96m (68ft 9in).
Weight empty: 11,083kg (24,465lb).
All-up weight: 15,800kg (34,880lb).
Maximum speed: 384km/h (239mph) at 7625m (25,000ft).
Maximum range: 3909km (2430 miles) 282km/h (175mph).
Service ceiling: 8479m (27,800ft).
Engines: Four 850hp Wright R-1829-39 radials.
Armament: Five 0.50 or 0.30in machine guns.
Maximum bomb load: 3624kg (8000lb).
Average bomb load: 1812kg (4000lb).

Y1B-17A (BOEING MODEL 229F)
Span: 31.12m (103ft 9in).
Length: 20.96m (68ft 9in).
Weight empty: 14,115kg (31,160lb).
All-up weight: 19.932kg (44,000lb).
Maximum speed: 436km/h (271mph) at 7625m (25,000ft).
Maximum range: Not known.
Service ceiling: 11,590m (38,000ft).
Engines: Four 1000hp Wright R-1820-51 radials.
Armament: Five 0.50 or 0.30in machine guns.
Maximum bomb load: 3624kg (8000lb).
Average bomb load: 1812kg (4000lb).

B-17B (BOEING MODEL 299M)
Span: 31.12m (103ft 9in).
Length: 20.67m (67ft 10in).
Weight empty: 12,526kg (27,652lb).
All-up weight: 17,213kg (37,997lb).
Maximum speed: 431km/h (268mph) at 7625m (25,000ft).
Maximum range: 4827km (3000 miles) at 365km/h (227mph).
Service ceiling: 10,370m (34,000ft).
Engines: Four 1000hp Wright R-1850-51 radials.
Armament: Two 0.30 and three 0.50 machine guns.
Maximum bomb load: 1812kg (4000lb).
Average bomb load: 906kg (2000lb).

B-17C (BOEING MODEL 299H)
Span: 31.12m (103ft 9in).
Length: 20.67m (67ft 10in).
Weight empty: 13,146kg (29,021lb).
All-up weight: 17,696kg (39,065lb).
Maximum speed: 482km/h (300mph).
Maximum range: 5470km (3400 miles) at 365km/h (227mph).
Service ceiling: 10,980m (36,000ft).
Engines: Four 1000hp Wright R-1820-65 radials.
Armament: Six 0.50 and one 0.30in machine guns.
Maximum bomb load: 1812kg (4000lb).
Average bomb load: 906kg (2000lb).

B-17D (BOEING MODEL 299H)
Span: 31.12m (103ft 9in).
Length: 20.67m (67ft 10in).
Weight empty: 14,026kg (30,963lb).
All-up weight: 17,811kg (39,319lb).
Maximum speed: 512km/h (318mph) at 7625m (25,000ft).
Maximum range: 4087km (2540 miles) at 365km/h (227mph).
Service ceiling: 11,529m (37,800ft).
Engines: Four 1000hp Wright R-1820-65 radials.
Armament: Six 0.50 and one 0.30in machine guns.
Maximum bomb load: 1812kg (4000lb).
Average bomb load: 906kg (2000lb).

B-17E (BOEING MODEL 299O)
Span: 31.12m (103ft 9in).
Length: 22.5m (73ft 10in).
Weight empty: 15,075kg (33,279lb).
All-up weight: 18,238kg (40,260lb).
Maximum speed: 512km/h (318mph) at 7625m (25,000ft).
Maximum range: 5309km (3300 miles) at 364km/h (226mph).
Service ceiling: 10,675m (35,000ft).
Engines: Four 1000hp Wright R-1820-91 radials.
Armament: Eight 0.50 and one 0.30in machine guns.
Maximum bomb load: 5798kg (12,800lb).
Average bomb load: 2718kg (6000lb).

B-17F (BOEING MODEL 299O)
Span: 31.12m (103ft 9in).
Length: 22.8m (74ft 9in).
Weight empty: 16,185kg (35,728lb).
All-up weight: 18,238kg (40,260lb).
Maximum speed: 523km/h (325mph) at 7625m (25,000ft).
Maximum range: 7112km (4420 miles) at 257km/h (160mph).
Service ceiling: 11,285m (37,000ft).
Engines: Four 1000hp Wright R-1820-65 radials.
Armament: Nine 0.50 and one 0.30in machine guns.
Maximum bomb load: 5798kg (12,800lb).
Average bomb load: 2718kg (6000lb).

B-17G (BOEING MODEL 299O CHIN TURRET)
Span: 31.12m (103ft 9in).
Length: 22.8m (74ft 9in).
Weight empty: 16,369kg (36,134lb).
All-up weight: 17,305kg (38,200lb).
Maximum speed: 486km/h (302mph) at 7625m (25,000ft).
Maximum range: 6034km (3750 miles) at 257km/h (160mph).
Service ceiling: 10,675m (35,000ft).
Engines: Four 1000hp Wright R-1820-97 radials.
Armament: Thirteen 0.50in MGs.
Maximum bomb load: 5798kg (12,800lb).
Average bomb load: 2718kg (6000lb).

externally similar to the B-17E in every respect. The differences – and there were hundreds of them – were internal, and included major improvements such as the addition of 'Tokyo' wing tanks to extend the aircraft's range.

Late production B-17Fs were fitted with a new chin turret, a legacy left behind by the ill-starred YB-40 'Fighter Fortress', described in Chapter Seven of this book, and this became standard on the next model and last major variant, the B-17G. The first B-17G was delivered on 4 September 1943 and the last on 13 April 1945, less than a month before the German surrender.

Left: A female factory worker wiring up the interior of a Flying Fortress. Wiring installations became more complex as the war progressed and the aircraft was fitted with new apparatus.

Below: Brand-new B-17Gs 'on the ramp' at Boeing's Seattle plant, ready for delivery to their units overseas. This shot shows a day's worth of production at the plant's peak – 16 B-17s.

B-17 PRODUCTION

In the summer of 1941, some four months before the Japanese attack on Pearl Harbor but with the political situation in the Pacific area deteriorating rapidly and the threat of war with Japan looming nearer, it was realised that the Flying Fortress would soon be needed in large numbers. The Air Corps consequently set up a production pool, combining the efforts of Boeing, the Douglas Aircraft Company and the Vega Division of Lockheed, to mass-produce the B-17, starting with the F model. All three companies had considerable experience in the production of bomber aircraft; Douglas was responsible for building the B-18 twin-engined monoplane bomber and the DB-7, the latter originally intended for service with the French Air Force, while Lockheed was producing the Hudson twin-engined maritime patrol bomber for the RAF. Production lines were quickly set up; tools and blueprints were supplied by Boeing, so that the Fortresses produced by all three companies were identical, except for very minor internal differences.

Variant	USAAC/USAAF Serials	Number Built	Variant	USAAC/USAAF Serials	Number Built
Y1B-17	36-149 to 36-161	13	B-17G	42-31032 to 42-32116	1084
				42-97058 to 42-97407	350
Y1B-17A	37-369	1		42-102379 to 42-102978	600
				43-37509 to 43-39508	2000
B-17B	38-211 to 38-223	13		42-3563	1
	38-258 to 38-270	13		Built by Douglas Aircraft	
	38-583 to 38-584	2		42-37716	1
	38-610	1		Built by Douglas aircraft	
	39-001 to 39-010	10		42-37721 to 42-38213	493
Total		**39**		Built by Douglas Aircraft	
				42-106984 to 42-107233	250
B-17C	40-2042 to 40-2079	38		Built by Douglas Aircraft	
				44-6001 to 44-7000	1000
B-17D	40-3059 to 40-3100	42		Built by Douglas Aircraft	
				44-83236 to 44-83885	650
B-17E	41-2393 to 41-2699	307		Built by Douglas Aircraft	
	41-9011 to 41-9245	235		42-39758 to 42-40057	300
Total		**512**		Built by Lockheed-Vega	
				42-97436 to 42-98035	600
B-17F	41-24340 to 41-24639	300		Built by Lockheed-Vega	
	42-5050 to 42-5484	435		44-8001 to 44-9000	1000
	42-29467 to 42-31031	1565		Built by Lockheed-Vega	
	42-2964 to 42-3562	599		44-85492 to 44-85841	350
	Built by Douglas Aircraft			Built by Lockheed-Vega	
	42-37714 to 42-37715	2	**Total**		**8679**
	Built by Douglas Aircraft				
	42-37717 to 42-37720	3	Total B-17 production all variants		12,731
	Built by Douglas Aircraft			(Including Model 299 prototype)	
	42-5705 to 42-6204	500			
	Built by Lockheed-Vega				
Total		**3404**	B-17 Sorties Flown in the European Theatre, 1942–45		291,508
			(B-24 Liberator)		(226,775)
			Bomb Tonnage Dropped		640,036
			(B-24 Liberator)		(452,508)
			Combat Losses		4688
			(B-24 Liberator)		(3626)

CHAPTER 3

B-17 Operations in the Pacific, 1941–43

The B-17 received its baptism of fire during the Japanese attack on Pearl Harbor, and although it was later superseded by the longer-range B-29 Superfortress, the Flying Fortress performed sterling service against the Japanese at a difficult stage of the war for the United States.

On 1 February 1940, the 11th Bombardment Group was activated in Hawaii, and spent the following months training on B-18s before being designated a Heavy Bombardment Group in November, pending the arrival of its first B-17s. The aircraft arrived in ones and twos, and shortly after their arrival they were stripped of their inadequate 0.30 calibre machine guns, which were replaced by more powerful hand-held 0.50 calibre weapons with a maximum range of about 1371m (4498ft). From their principal base at Hickam Field, 11th BG B-17s ranged far and wide on training profiles across the Pacific, one of their main destinations being Clark Field in the Philippines, headquarters of the US Far East Air Force under Major General Lewis H. Brereton. A second B-17 group – the 19th Bombardment Group (Heavy) – was activated at Clark in September 1941.

A third group, the 7th, was also assigned to the Philippines, and on 7 December 1941 a dozen brand-new B-17s of this unit, en route to the Philippines, literally flew into the middle of a shooting war when they approached Hickam Field to refuel at the height of the Japanese attack on Pearl Harbor. The Fortresses were unarmed, their guns having been removed to reduce weight and so conserve fuel.

Major Richard H. Carmichael, leading the first flight of six B-17s, sighted columns of smoke rising from Hickam as he approached the field at the end of a 14-hour flight and decided to divert to Bellows Field, only to find that it, too, was under attack. In the end he landed at Haleiwa, a small fighter

Left: Hickam Field after the Japanese surprise attack of 7 December 1941. The aircraft in the foreground is a newly arrived B-17E; behind is a B-17D. Stores are still burning in the background.

strip, followed by another B-17. A third aircraft, piloted by Lieutenant Frank Bostrum, set down on a golf course near Hickam – an astonishing feat of airmanship – and the remaining three managed to land at Hickam during the first two Japanese attack waves.

Shortly afterwards the second B-17 flight, led by Major Truman H. Landon, arrived over Hickam just as the second enemy attack was beginning to develop; four B-17s landed safely, but a fifth was shot up as it touched down and broke in half. Japanese fighters strafed the crew as they ran from the wreck, killing one man (Flight Surgeon William R. Shick). The sixth aircraft, surviving an attack that severely wounded two crew members, landed at Bellows Field. All these B-17s, together with ten more 7th BG aircraft that reached Hawaii a few days later, remained there and were assigned to antisubmarine patrol duties.

At the time of the Japanese attack there were 35 19th Group B-17s based in the Philippines, comprising two squadrons with 19 aircraft at Clark and two with 16 aircraft at Del Monte on Mindanao. The American war plan, in the event of hostilities between Japan and the USA, envisaged attacks by the Philippines-based bombers on enemy targets (primarily naval bases) on Formosa, but for political considerations – the Philippine Government was still neutral – no authorisation to bomb up the B-17s was issued. On his own initiative, Major David Gibbs, operations officer of the 19th BG and in temporary command while the Group

Commander, Lieutenant-Colonel Eugene L. Eubank, was at General Brereton's HQ, ordered every available B-17 to patrol the seas around Luzon until recalled to Clark. When Eubank came back, he recalled the B-17s and ordered them to be bombed up in readiness for offensive action; he also ordered three B-17s to depart on a reconnaissance mission to Formosa.

The first of these aircraft was taxying out shortly after midday on 8 December when the Japanese attacked Clark Field. High-level bombers struck first, followed by dive-bombers and then strafing fighters. When the attack ended, not one B-17 at Clark was in an airworthy condition.

DEL MONTE FORTRESSES

General Brereton's offensive capability now rested on the B-17s at Del Monte, 966km (600 miles) to the south of Clark Field. Japanese reconnaissance had not yet detected them, and in any case they were outside the combat radius of the enemy's Formosa-based Zero fighters. By 9 December reconnaissance missions were being flown by aircraft of the 19th Group, the B-17s carrying limited bomb loads in case enemy ships were sighted. Five aircraft were involved, led by Major Cecil E. Combs, commanding the 93rd Squadron, and on the 10th this pilot led five Fortresses, each carrying 20 45kg

Below: Another view of the devastation at Hickam. Fortresses of the 7th Bomb Group arrived while the Japanese attack was in progress. Amazingly, most survived the experience.

Above: The Boeing B-17D was the last variant to feature this type of tail configuration, and served largely in the Pacific. The more familiar Fortress tail was introduced with the B-17E.

(100lb) bombs, into action against a large enemy convoy that had been sighted off Vigan. In the ensuing attack the Japanese minesweeper *W19* was hit and had to be beached. In another mission two B-17s of the 14th Squadron set out to attack enemy shipping at Appari and a third, flown by Lt G.R. Montgomery, was sent to Vigan. On the return flight Montgomery ran into severe weather and was forced to ditch, but all the crew members were rescued. Another aircraft, flown by Captain Colin B. Kelly, was attacked by Zeros; a B-17C, it was not fitted with self-sealing fuel tanks and was soon ablaze. Kelly got his crew out safely, but was killed when the B-17 exploded in mid-air.

On 14 December six B-17s were despatched to Legaspi to attack Japanese forces landing there. One aircraft burst a tyre on take-off and two were forced to return to Del Monte with technical problems; the other three pressed on and two attacked the enemy beachhead. One B-17 (Lt Jack Adams) was shot up by Zeros and had to make a forced landing in a paddy field on Masbate Island and another (Lt Hewitt T. Wheless), reduced to little more than a flying wreck by fighter attacks that persisted until the enemy's ammunition ran out, made an emergency landing on an airstrip at Cagayan. The crew all escaped, and later counted 1200 bullet holes in their aircraft.

Of the 35 B-17s that had been in the Philippines when the Japanese attacked, only 14 remained at Del Monte, and it was decided that these – along with what little else remained of the Far East Air Force – should be evacuated to Australia. On December 17, the first B-17s made the 2413km (1500-mile) flight to Batchelor Field, near Darwin. Forty-eight hours later Del Monte was subjected to its first air attack, but the remaining B-17s were well camouflaged and escaped damage. By 24 December all had been flown to Australia.

ATTACK ON DAVAO

Two days earlier, on the 22nd, nine B-17s – all available aircraft – took off to attack Davao in the southern Philippines,

where a Japanese landing had just taken place. This attack, and others on Japanese forces at Lingayen Gulf, produced no tangible result, and by 25 December only three Fortresses remained serviceable at Batchelor Field. New aircraft – B-17Es of the 7th Bombardment Group, refugees from Hawaii – began to trickle in, but these scant reinforcements did little to redress the situation.

Of the original B-17s that served at Clark Field, only one was to survive. A B-17D, it was literally a hybrid, made up of parts cannibalised from other wrecked B-17s. One of its pilots, Weldon H. Smith, named it 'Alexander the Swoose' after a popular song of the day telling of a creature that was half swan, half goose.

In Java, a dwindling force of 7th and 19th Group B-17s continued to operate right up to the final evacuation. On 11 February 1942, 15 Fortresses and four LB-30s (the export version of the B-24 Liberator) assembled to attack Japanese forces at Palembang, the location of a major oil refinery and a primary Japanese objective, but a sudden air raid alert forced the bombers to take off hurriedly in order to escape destruction on the ground and the attack was cancelled. On the 13th another force of 14 bombers was assembled to attack an enemy convoy, but the ships were not sighted. By the next morning only eight B-17s remained serviceable, and the surviving aircraft were used to evacuate American personnel from Java to the airstrip at Broome, on the northwest coast of Australia. On 3 March the airstrip was attacked by nine Zeros operating from Timor, captured a few days earlier; aircraft destroyed included two B-17Es, further depleting the Americans' offensive capability.

THE BATTLE OF THE CORAL SEA

Early in May 1942 B-17s of the 19th BG flew reconnaissance missions in support of Allied naval forces in action against a Japanese invasion force heading for Port Moresby, New Guinea. This action, which became known as the Battle of the Coral Sea, thwarted the Japanese invasion attempt but cost the Americans the aircraft carrier USS *Lexington* sunk and another, the *Yorktown*, damaged. But two Japanese fleet carriers, the *Shokaku* and *Zuikaku*, had also been so badly damaged that they would be out of action for two months.

Their absence was to cost the Japanese dearly in another strategically vital battle that took place just a month after the combat in the Coral Sea.

In Hawaii, the 11th Bombardment Group had recovered from the losses inflicted on it during the Pearl Harbor attack. It was now part of the Seventh Air Force, and in March 1942 it had acquired a new commander, Colonel LaVerne G. 'Blondie' Saunders, a West Point graduate who had immediately embarked on a rigorous training schedule. As a result of all this effort, the 11th BG was combat-ready when, at the end of May 1942, intelligence was received that the Japanese were planning an invasion of Midway Island.

Colonel Saunders at once authorised the despatch of 17 Fortresses to the island, the first eight aircraft leaving Hawaii on 30 May and the rest the day after. The whole striking force was under the command of Lt Col Walter C. Sweeney, a rather flamboyant character, who named his Flying Fortress

'Knucklehead' and flew it wearing nothing more on his feet than his socks.

On 3 June the Japanese invasion force was sighted by a Navy PBY Catalina, and at 1230 hours Sweeney's Fortresses took off to attack it, each aircraft carrying maximum fuel and a reduced bomb load of 272kg (600lb). At 1623 a large number of Japanese transport vessels came into sight and the Fortresses made their bombing runs at altitudes varying from 2440 to 3660m (8000 to 12,000ft). Some of the crew thought that they had hit their targets, reporting that some ships had been left on fire, but in fact none of the enemy vessels was touched; the smoke came from screens laid down by escorting warships.

MIDWAY

The next morning, Sweeney led a 15-strong force of B-17s from Midway at dawn to make a second attack on the invasion transports, but soon after becoming airborne he received a new target: the aircraft carriers *Akagi*, *Kaga*, *Hiryu* and *Soryu*, whose aircraft had the task of destroying what was left of the US Pacific Fleet when it was brought to

Below: Waist gunners in a B-17. Manning the hand-held guns was a difficult operation, and accurate aiming was almost impossible. Later models staggered the guns to give the gunners more room to move.

Above: Armourers cleaning a B-17's guns. The Fortress' armament was quickly increased from five 0.50in or 0.30in weapons to nine 0.50s and one 0.30. The last variant, the B-17G, had 13 0.50s.

battle in the defence of Midway. The B-17 crews positively identified the *Soryu* and *Hiryu* and duly made their attack, again claiming hits, but no bombs found their mark; the destruction of all four enemy carriers was brought about by US naval aircraft, their crews well trained in the dive-bombing and torpedo attack roles.

With the Battle of Midway over, Sweeney's B-17s returned to Hawaii. In July 1942 the 11th Bombardment Group was assigned to the Thirteenth Air Force and, designated as the Mobile Force Central Pacific, was ordered to move up to New Caledonia. The 98th Squadron was the first to move, reaching its new home – Plaines des Gaiacs – in a torrential rainstorm on 22 July. The 42nd Squadron arrived the next day, and on the 24th the 431st Squadron deployed to Nadi, in the Fiji Islands. The fourth squadron of the 11th BG, the 26th, deployed to Efate in the New Hebrides on the 25th.

On the following day – 26 July – the 26th Squadron under the command of Major Allan J. Stewart moved forward to Espiritu Santo, the northernmost island of that group, to begin operations against the Japanese as part of a softening-up bombardment prior to the invasion of Guadalcanal, the first stepping stone on the long Central Pacific road whose terminus was Japan itself. Beginning on 31 July, the squadrons of the 11th BG flew 56 bombing sorties and 22 sea-search sorties. The longest-range missions were attacks flown from Efate, which was 1316km (710nm) from the nearest point on Guadalcanal, so that once again bomb loads had to be sacrificed for an increased fuel uplift.

Matters improved after 1 August, when the Espiritu Santo strip became fully operational; this enabled the B-17s to carry full bomb loads to the target and refuel at Espiritu on the way back to Efate. Occasionally, enemy fighters – all

THE SAGA OF THE SWOOSE

'The Swoose', serial number 40-3097, was a 19th Bombardment Group aircraft and was in the thick of the fighting, operating out of Batchelor Field and later out of Java before the Japanese overran that also. Evacuated to Australia, The Swoose was virtually rebuilt at the end of its combat career; for example, it acquired a tail unit salvaged from an aircraft flown by Lt George E. Schaetzel that was so riddled with Japanese cannon shells and bullets that the tail was just about the only thing worth saving. Assigned to VIP transport duties, The Swoose was eventually requisitioned by General George H. Brett, commanding the US Army forces in Australia, and it subsequently carried some very important passengers – including a tall, lanky Congressman from Texas, then on active service as a lieutenant commander in the US Navy. His name was Lyndon B. Johnson, and he was on board the aircraft when it had to make a forced landing in the outback as the result of a compass error on a flight from Darwin to Cloncurry.

When General Brett was appointed to the Caribbean Defense Command in the summer of 1942 The Swoose went with him, making the flight from Australia to Washington DC in the record time of 36 hours. Its pilot was Colonel Frank Kurz, a former Olympic diving star who later named his daughter (who was herself to become a celebrity as a stage star on Broadway) 'Swoosie'.

Her active service days over, The Swoose was donated to the Smithsonian Institution's National Air Museum, restored and placed in storage at the Douglas Aircraft factory at Old Orchard Airport, now Chicago's O'Hare International Airport. The famous B-17 remains part of the Smithsonian collection and is now in storage at Silver Hill, Maryland.

Nakajima A6M2 'Rufe' floatplanes – were encountered during bombing raids on enemy installations on Tulagi, another island in the Solomons; the Rufes, which belonged to the Yokohama Kokutai (Wing) had deployed there some weeks earlier. They shot down a B-17 and possibly accounted for a second, which went missing on reconnaissance on the day the Guadalcanal invasion was scheduled to take place. A third B-17 was also lost when it collided with a Rufe during an attack on Lunga airfield. Three Rufes were shot down by B-17 gunners, and the rest were destroyed on the ground in the Fortresses' bombing campaign.

The Japanese made desperate attempts to recapture Guadalcanal, precipitating a series of hard-fought actions that collectively became known as the Battle of the Eastern

Inside the B-17 Flying Fortress

The B-17 was a complex piece of machinery primarily designed to deliver bombs over long ranges. It was not a comfortable place for its ten crew members during the lengthy missions they performed over Germany and elsewhere, but by the last year of the war it was at least bristling with machine guns to fend off the Luftwaffe's attacks.

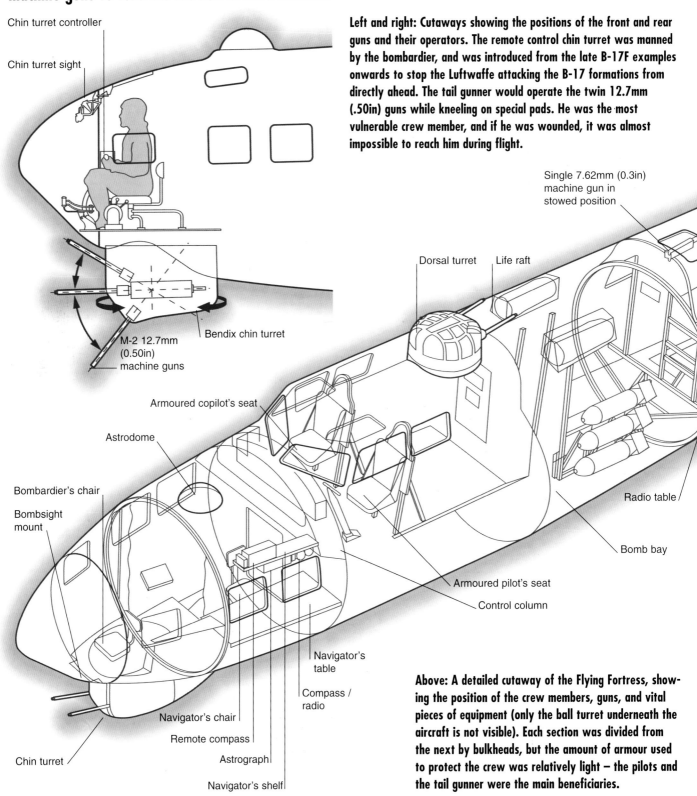

Chin turret controller

Chin turret sight

Left and right: Cutaways showing the positions of the front and rear guns and their operators. The remote control chin turret was manned by the bombardier, and was introduced from the late B-17F examples onwards to stop the Luftwaffe attacking the B-17 formations from directly ahead. The tail gunner would operate the twin 12.7mm (.50in) guns while kneeling on special pads. He was the most vulnerable crew member, and if he was wounded, it was almost impossible to reach him during flight.

Single 7.62mm (0.3in) machine gun in stowed position

Dorsal turret   Life raft

M-2 12.7mm (0.50in) machine guns

Bendix chin turret

Armoured copilot's seat

Astrodome

Radio table

Bombardier's chair

Bombsight mount

Bomb bay

Armoured pilot's seat

Control column

Navigator's table

Chin turret

Navigator's chair

Remote compass

Astrograph

Compass / radio

Navigator's shelf

Above: A detailed cutaway of the Flying Fortress, showing the position of the crew members, guns, and vital pieces of equipment (only the ball turret underneath the aircraft is not visible). Each section was divided from the next by bulkheads, but the amount of armour used to protect the crew was relatively light – the pilots and the tail gunner were the main beneficiaries.

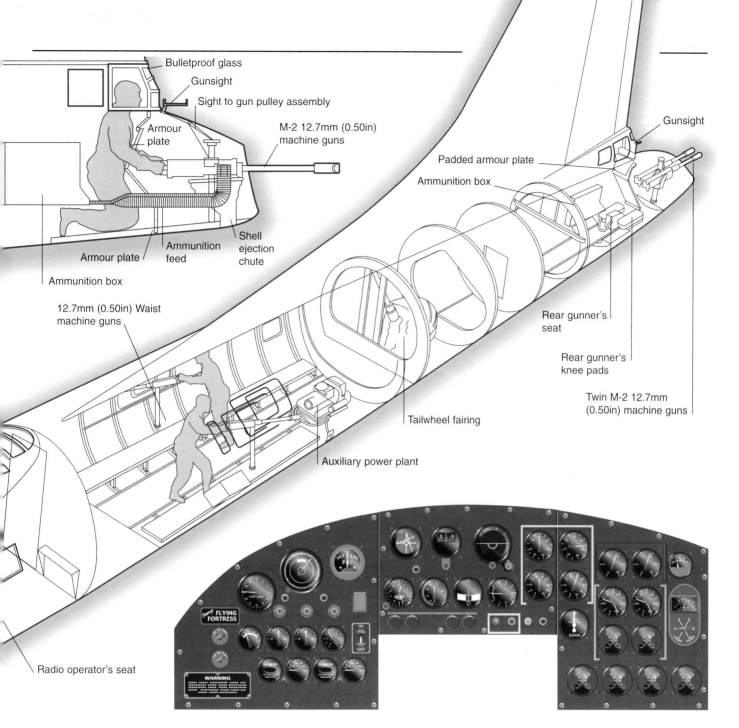

Bulletproof glass

Gunsight

Sight to gun pulley assembly

Armour plate

M-2 12.7mm (0.50in) machine guns

Armour plate

Ammunition feed

Shell ejection chute

Ammunition box

12.7mm (0.50in) Waist machine guns

Padded armour plate

Ammunition box

Gunsight

Rear gunner's seat

Rear gunner's knee pads

Twin M-2 12.7mm (0.50in) machine guns

Tailwheel fairing

Auxiliary power plant

Radio operator's seat

FLYING FORTRESS

WARNING

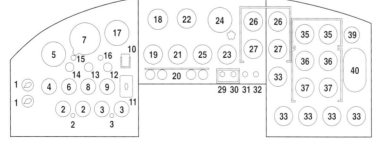

Right: The instrument panel of the B-17 Flying Fortress, showing the array of gauges, switches and lights facing the two pilots and their functions. Although the USAAF flew daylight missions, cloud or a late return to base could force the pilots to fly by instruments alone.

1. Fluorescent light switches
2. Pilot's oxygen controls
3. Copilot's oxygen controls
4. Voltmeter
5. Radio compass
6. Emergency oil pressure gauge
7. Flux gate compass
8. Hydraulic oil pressure
9. Suction gauge
10. Altimeter correction card
11. Airspeed alternate source
12. Vacuum warning light
13. Main hydraulic oil warning light
14. Emergency hydraulic oil warning light
15. Bomb door position light
16. Bomb release light
17. Pilot's directional indicator
18. Pilot's localiser indicator
19. Altimeter
20. Propeller feathering switches
21. Airspeed indicator
22. Directional gyro
23. Rate-of-climb indicator
24. Flight indicator
25. Turn-and-bank indicator
26. Manifold pressure
27. Tachometers
28. Marker beacon light
29. Globe test button
30. Bomber call light
31. Landing gear warning light
32. Tailwheel lock light
33. Flap position indicator
34. Cylinder-head temperatures
35. Fuel pressure
36. Oil pressure
37. Oil temperature
38. Carburetor air temperature
39. Free air temperature
40. Fuel quantity

Solomons. On the night of 18/19 August Japanese destroyers landed a force of some 900 men east of the American bridge-head on Guadalcanal, held by the 1st US Marine Division. When the Japanese force attacked it was annihilated, and the next morning the destroyers *Kagero*, *Hagikaze* and *Maikaze* were attacked by B-17s from Espiritu Santo. *Hagikaze* was badly damaged by bomb hits and had to be escorted away by *Maikaze*. (The Americans believed at the time that *Hagikaze* was a light cruiser, and that she had been sunk; in fact, she returned to combat after repairs and was not sunk until August 1943.)

GUADALCANAL

In the last week of August 1942 a major air and sea battle developed east of the Solomons as the Japanese attempted to land 1500 men on Guadalcanal under cover of the Combined Fleet. A diversionary force, comprising the light aircraft car-rier *Ryujo*, a cruiser and two destroyers, was sighted on 24 August and immediately attacked by carrier aircraft from the USS *Saratoga*. The first strike damaged the *Ryujo*, and while under tow she was attacked by 11th BG B-17s, which claimed to have scored four hits on her. She was finished off

Above: B-17F 41-24457 over the Pacific islands. By the early months of 1943, most B-17s had been returned to the USA for assignment to the Eighth Air Force's combat groups in Britain.

later by carrier aircraft, which also damaged the cruiser *Tone*. Later in the day the B-17s were in action against enemy resupply ships, claiming two hits on a large freighter. During this mission a flight of four B-17s was heavily attacked by Zero fighters, which damaged two of the Fortresses, one of which crashed into a hillside while attempting a night land-ing at Espiritu Santo. The Fortress gunners claimed four Zeros destroyed and seven damaged.

While the 11th BG was active in the Solomons, the 19th BG, now based on Mareeba in Queensland, northeastern Australia, was attacking targets on the Japanese-occupied island of Rabaul in the New Britain group, where the enemy had established several important air bases. The 19th BG formed part of the newly activated Fifth Air Force, com-manded by Major George C. Kenney; the Group was finally relieved in the late summer of 1942 and sent back to the United States. During its active service in the Pacific the exploits of its crews had earned one Medal of Honor

(awarded to Lt Harl Pease for pressing home an attack on the enemy airfield at Vunakanau while under heavy fighter attack) and seven Distinguished Unit Citations, among many other awards. The 19th would return to the Pacific later in the war, as a Very Heavy Group armed with Boeing B-29s.

Its replacement in the Fifth Air Force was the 43rd Bombardment Group, which, after a period of anti-submarine patrol duty off the coast of New England, was ordered to Australia via Cape Town. The 43rd was soon in action against a wide range of enemy targets in the Dutch East Indies and the Bismarck Sea area; for anti-shipping operations it practised 'skip-bombing', in which a bomb released during a low-level attack would bounce off the surface of the water and into the side of its target, like a flat stone skipping over the surface of a pond.

The 43rd BG particularly distinguished itself in the Battle of the Bismarck Sea early in March 1943, when eight Japanese transports and a similar number of destroyers attempted to land 6900 troops of the Japanese 51st Division at Lae, in New Guinea. Sighted by a B-24 Liberator reconnaissance aircraft early on 2 March northeast of Dampier Strait, the convoy was attacked two hours later by 12 43rd

BG Fortresses, which sank a large transport and damaged two more. On the following day B-17s joined some 350 other American and Australian aircraft in low-level attacks on the convoy as it entered the Bismarck Sea; all the transports and four destroyers were sunk.

On 16 June 1943 a lone 43rd BG B-17 was sent out to make a reconnaissance of Buka airstrip near Bougainville, in the Solomon Islands. Flying at 8540m (28,000ft), with about 16km (10 miles) to run to the target, the unescorted Fortress was savagely attacked by about 20 Zeros and, despite the best efforts of the gunners, the aircraft began taking hits. The main oxygen system was put out of action and the pilot, Major Jay Zeamer, was forced to decend to a lower altitude. The bombardier, Lt Joseph R. Sarnoski, was manning the nose gun position when a shell exploded in his compartment, blasting him into the catwalk beneath the pilots' cockpit and wounding him in the stomach. Despite his injuries, he crawled back to his gun and fired off another burst or two before collapsing, lifeless.

Major Zeamer, meanwhile, had been hit in the legs and one arm and only two crew members – the tail gunner and the photographer – were still unwounded. The battle raged for 40 minutes, during which the B-17 completed its mission and turned for home – the airfield at Dobodura in New Guinea, 965km (600 miles) away.

The crew members who could still function faced a critical situation. The flap controls, compass, radio and brakes were all out of action, the two pilots had fainted through loss of blood, and the navigator was also wounded. On his own initiative, top turret gunner John Able took over the controls and flew the aircraft by instinct. From time to time Zeamer and co-pilot John Britton recovered sufficiently to assist him, and together they managed to steer the aircraft back to base. While Britton, who had been hit in the arms, used his feet on the rudder pedals, Zeamer operated the control wheel with his one good hand, and somehow they made a successful landing – albeit downwind, the Fortress using up all the runway before it came to a stop. Zeamer and Sarnoski were both awarded the Medal of Honor for their part in the mission, the latter posthumously; all the other crew members received the Distinguished Flying Cross.

THE END OF THE ROAD

By this time, the days of the B-17 in the Pacific Theatre were numbered. The few remaining aircraft of the 7th Bombardment Group had been assigned to the China-Burma-India Theatre in 1942; the 19th BG had returned to the USA a few months later; and the 11th BG had ceased operations in the Pacific in March 1943, returning to Hawaii to re-equip with the B-24 Liberator. This was the aircraft, with its very long range, that would now lead the bombing offensive in the Pacific. No more B-17s would be assigned to the theatre. They were needed elsewhere, in skies where the B-17 was to fight its greatest and most costly battles.

CHAPTER 4

Operations in Northwest Europe, 1942–44

One of the most enduring images of World War II is that of rows of B-17 Flying Fortresses parked next to each other on East Anglian airfields, waiting for the next raid on Hitler's Reich to begin. It was here that the B-17 made its name as a weapon of war.

Following a great deal of groundwork by a small group of American officers led by General Ira C. Eaker in the early months of 1942, involving among other things the setting up of a headquarters for the newly formed 8th Bomber Command at High Wycombe, in Buckinghamshire, the first Flying Fortress to be deployed to the European Theatre, a B-17E serial number 19085, touched down at Prestwick in Scotland on 1 July that year. It was the vanguard of the 97th Bombardment Group (340th, 341st, 342nd and 414th Squadrons), which deployed 38 B-17s to its British airfields of Polebrook and Grafton between 6 and 31 July 1942.

On 15 August 1942, 24 crews of the 97th BG were alerted to carry out the first American bombing attack from Britain, with fighter cover provided by the Spitfire squadrons of No 11 Group, RAF Fighter Command. After a delay caused by poor weather, the mission took place on 17 August, the target being the marshalling yards at Rouen. Twelve B-17s took part in the attack, with six more acting as a diversionary force along the French coast. The bombing, carried out in good weather conditions, achieved good results, and only one B-17 received slight flak damage. On 19 August two B-17s (out of 24 despatched) bombed the German fighter airfield at Abbeville; all returned safely to base.

The build-up of B-17s in Britain – known as Operation Bolero – continued throughout the late summer of 1942, although at a slower rate than General Eaker would have wished. The second group to arrive, beginning on 9 August 1942, was the 301st (32nd, 352nd, 353rd and 419th

Left: Mission accomplished: silhouetted against the rays of the dying sun, a B-17 is about to land at an English airfield. Nearly 4700 never came back from operations over Europe.

Squadrons), which brought its new B-17Fs to Chelveston and began operations on 5 September, making an unsuccessful attack on Rouen. On 18 August the 92nd BG (325th, 326th, 327th and 407th Squadrons) began arriving at Alconbury, and in September the 305th BG (364th, 365th, 366th and 422nd Squadrons) and the 306th BG (367th, 368th, 369th and 423rd Squadrons) became respectively established at Bovington and Thurleigh. By November 1942 the 91st BG (322nd, 323rd, 324th and 401st Squadrons) and the 303rd BG (358th, 359th, 360th and 427th Squadrons) were also operational at the Cambridgeshire airfields of Kimbolton and Molesworth, and during the rest of the year the American daylight bombers carried out many more attacks on targets in France and the Low Countries, all within range of fighter escort.

THE FIRST DAYLIGHT OFFENSIVE

American plans to attack targets in Germany were delayed for a variety of reasons, mainly the lack of fighter escort and the Allied landings in North Africa, which helped to set back the Eighth Air Force's build-up in Britain because of the pressing need for heavy bombers in the Mediterranean Theatre. But at the beginning of January 1943 General Eaker had 500 B-17s and B-24s under his command, and he judged that the time was ripe for the big daylight offensive to begin.

Below: The Norden bombsight, which gave the bombardier complete control of the aircraft during its bombing run, and automatically released the bombs at the calculated optimum moment.

There was little doubt in the minds of the Allied commanders that 1943 would be the decisive year in the war, the year in which the Allies, as the enemy was well aware, would attempt an invasion of Occupied Europe. Where the blow would fall no one yet knew, not even the Allies themselves, for the policy governing the conduct of the war in Europe at the close of the North African campaign had yet to be determined by the Allied leaders.

It was for this purpose that a top-level conference between President Roosevelt, Prime Minister Winston Churchill and the combined Allied Chiefs of Staff was held at Casablanca in January 1943. One of the decisions reached by the Allied leaders was to weld the strategic bombing arms of the Royal Air Force and United States Army Air Force into a single mighty weapon whose task would be, in the words of the resulting Directive, 'the progressive destruction and dislocation of the German military, industrial and economic system, and the undermining of the morale of the German people to a point where their capacity for armed resistance is fatally weakened.'

The Americans believed that they could best fulfil the demands of the Casablanca Directive by carrying out concentrated daylight attacks on six principal target systems, designed to achieve the maximum destruction in selected major industries. These systems were, in order of priority, submarine construction yards and bases, the aircraft industry, the ball-bearing industry, oil production, synthetic rubber production and factories producing military transport. The

target selected for the first American raid on Germany was one that fell within the leading category of objectives; the big naval base at Wilhelmshaven, a major centre of U-boat production. During the last week of January 1943 air reconnaissance revealed that the production yards were in full swing and that, as an additional bonus, the battleship *Admiral Scheer* was in dry dock.

On the morning of 27 January, 55 B-17s took off from their English bases and set course over the North Sea. The weather was far from ideal for high-level precision bombing, and at altitude the cold was intense. The sub-zero temperatures knifed through the thickest flying clothing; machine guns, turrets and camera mechanisms froze, while windscreens

Above: The B-17E bore the brunt of early Eighth Air Force operations over northwest Europe. Over 500 examples of this variant were built. The first arrived in England with the 97th BG in July 1942.

and bomb sights were obscured by opaque layers of frost. One of the navigators described the outward flight:

'At about 10.30 the altimeter indicated 25,000 feet. The cloud cover had ended, far below, and we could see the surface of the sea – like a sheet of glass. At 10.45 the Captain

Below: B-17E of the 97th BG, European Theatre of Operations, summer 1942. The aircraft has the 'scalloped' camouflage demarcation typical of this period, and still carries the 'US ARMY' legend.

warned the crew to be extra alert. I looked out to the right and could see the outline of the coast of Germany and the row of islands that lay just off it. At 10.57 we were just over the islands and at 11.00 the tail gunner reported flak at six o'clock, below. It was from the coastal islands and was the first time we were fired on from German soil. At this time we were beginning to turn and we crossed the island of Baltrum and went into German territory. As we turned, the bombardier elevated the muzzle of his gun and fired a burst so that the tracers arched over into Germany. The first shots from our ship, *Hell's Angel*, but not the last!'

The American raid took the German defences by surprise. Fifty-three Fortresses unloaded their bombs on the Wilhelmshaven harbour installations, opposed by only a handful of Focke-Wulf 190s; two more Fortresses bombed Emden. Only three B-17s failed to return, appearing to vindicate the Americans' belief that fears for the success of unescorted long-range daylight operations were unfounded. It would not be long before packs of determined Luftwaffe fighter pilots shattered the myth.

WEATHER DIFFICULTIES

In the days that followed the Wilhelmshaven mission, however, it was the weather and not the Luftwaffe that formed the main obstacle to the daylight bombing programme, with rain, sleet and dense cloud cover extending over the whole area of the North Sea. In 17 days only one attack was carried out, in conditions of severe icing and sub-zero temperatures. The raid took place on 4 February, and the target was the port of Emden. Because of the freezing conditions dense contrails formed behind the American formation at a much lower altitude than usual, enabling the enemy fighters to concentrate on it without difficulty. Fifty fighters, including eight Me 110s of a night fighter unit, engaged the bombers over the north coast of Germany and a fierce air battle developed. Six Fortresses were shot down but the Germans also suffered heavily, losing eight fighters.

On 16 February eight more bombers were lost during an attack on the locks leading to the basin of the St Nazaire U-boat base on the French coast. Ten days later another 8th Bomber Command formation battled its way through intense opposition to attack Wilhelmshaven for a second time. Seven bombers were lost.

Despite the losses suffered in these early raids, it was decided early in March to carry out the first of 8th Bomber Command's deep-penetration missions against a German objective. On the 4th, four Groups took off from their English bases to attack the big railway marshalling yards at Hamm, a target that had been frequently visited by the RAF in its programme of night-time raids. The operation was hampered by bad weather; two of the Groups bombed the shipyards at Rotterdam, another returned to base with its bombs still on board, and only the 91st BG – consisting of 16 bombers in total – reached the target. This lone Group achieved an excellent bombing concentration, but four of its aircraft were shot down in the operation.

Below: A tragic accident was the cause of this damage to a Flying Fortress: a bomb, dropped whilst being loaded into the bomb bay, exploded and broke the aircraft in two.

Above: Hit by flak in its starboard inner engine, a B-17 struggles to maintain formation. Stragglers were easy prey for enemy fighters, and many Fortresses were lost when they fell behind.

The next four missions were all against rail targets, including the marshalling yards at Rennes, hit by 50 B-17s on 8 March. Then, on the 18th, came the biggest raid so far, when 97 heavy bombers – 73 Fortresses and 24 B-24 Liberators, the largest force that 8th Bomber Command had yet sent out to strike at one target – attacked the Vulcan shipbuilding yards at Vegesack, on the river Weser south of Bremen. A B-17 bombardier, Lieutenant Jack Mathis of the 359th Squadron, 303rd Bombardment Group, gallantly remained at his post during the run-up to the target, although mortally wounded; he was awarded a posthumous Medal of Honor. The next day Wilhelmshaven was once again the target, followed in quick succession by the marshalling yards and repair shops at Rouen and the shipyards at Rotterdam. Eight bombers failed to return from these three missions, the last two of which were strongly escorted by Spitfires and Thunderbolts.

RAID ON RENAULT

The next objective slated for a major attack by the Eighth Air Force was the Renault works, in the suburbs of Paris. This target, wrecked by RAF Bomber Command on the night of 3/4 March 1942, had been completely rebuilt by the Germans in nine months – using French money and labour – and was now turning out 1500 tanks and trucks per month for the Wehrmacht, which represented ten per cent of the enemy's total production in this field.

At 1350 on 4 April 1943, 85 B-17s crossed Dieppe at 7625m (25,000ft) en route to Paris, clearly visible as a dark patch nestling in the loops of the Seine some 160km (95 miles) to the south. At 1400 the Spitfire escort turned back, at the limit of its combat radius, but as the Fortresses flew on unescorted there was still no sign of any enemy fighters; the Luftwaffe had been lured north by three diversionary attacks, mounted by No 2 Group RAF Bomber Command. At 1414 the B-17s were over the target, and in the next seven minutes the Groups dropped 255 tonnes (251 tons) of high explosive on it. Enemy fighters appeared for the first time as the bombers swung north towards the coast, and determined attacks persisted until the B-17s made rendezvous with more Spitfire squadrons over Rouen. Four bombers were lost, but reconnaissance showed that the Renault factory had once again been devastated.

The Eighth Air Force's raids continued to grow in size, and in cost. On 17 April, 115 B-17s took off to attack the Focke-Wulf aircraft factory at Bremen. Eight bombers aborted, but the remaining 107 battled their way to the target through fierce opposition. Sixteen B-17s failed to return, making this the costliest mission so far for the Americans.

By this time two factors – both by-products of the weather over western Europe – were beginning to hamper daylight

Left: B-17F 42-30793 *Tom Paine* of the 562nd Squadron, 388th Bomb Group. Operating from Knettishall in Suffolk, the 388th BG flew 8051 combat missions in World War II.

Above: Formation of B-17s en route to a target in Europe. This photograph clearly shows the defensive box formation adopted by the 8th Air Force, enabling each bomber to give its neighbours fire support.

operations to a noticeable extent. First of all, in early spring the days were still not long enough to permit the American crews – who were not trained for night operations – to attack targets in Germany outside a limited period midway between dawn and dusk. This period usually tended to coincide with maximum cloud development in the target area, so that visual identification of the target became a problem. Secondly, and for the same reason, the Germans were able to calculate the probable time of an American attack quite accurately and assemble their fighters accordingly. The latter needed to be on alert only from about three hours after sunrise to about three hours before sunset. The end result was that the Americans met with stronger opposition than ever before during April and May 1943, and their losses rose to a serious level.

SIMULTANEOUS ATTACKS

By the middle of May 1943 the Eighth Air Force had sufficient aircraft and crews operational in England to carry out a long awaited experiment: the mounting of simultaneous large-scale attacks on several targets. The first such mission took place on 14 May, when over 200 Fortresses and Liberators were despatched in the space of four hours to

attack Ijmuiden, Antwerp, Courtrai and Kiel. The diversity of the attacks caused some confusion among the German fighter controllers; nevertheless, the Luftwaffe hotly contested the Kiel attack, which was by far the biggest of the four, and six B-17s and five B-24s were lost.

In June 1943 the Combined Chiefs of Staff issued their directive for the start of Operation Pointblank, the joint round-the-clock Anglo-American bombing offensive against Germany's war industries. In terms of offensive power the Eighth Air Force was well equipped to undertake such a mission; by the beginning of July its strength had increased to 15 bomber groups comprising more than 300 B-17s and B-24s. The biggest obstacle to the success of deep-penetration daylight missions remained the lack of long-range fighter escort. In an effort to fill this critical gap the Americans slung droptanks under the wings of their Thunderbolts and Lightnings, which enabled them to penetrate as far as Germany's western frontier, but this did not provide a real solution.

On 28 July 1943 Thunderbolts escorted 77 Fortresses in two formations as far as the German frontier before turning back. The bombers flew on towards their targets, the Fieseler aircraft factory at Kassel-Bettenhausen and the AGO factories at Oschersleben, near Magdeburg. Enemy fighters engaged

Above: B-17s attacking an enemy airfield. As American losses increased, attacks on fighter airfields and centres of aircraft production became of vital importance, as did attacks on fuel production.

the B-17s from the moment they crossed the border, and one unit – II/JG2 – employed a novel attack technique: its Messerschmitts flew at 915m (3000ft) above the bombers and dropped 220kg (500lb) bombs on them. Three bombers in one formation were destroyed by this means. The remainder scattered, and the Messerschmitts pounced. II/JG2 alone destroyed 11 bombers, and the total American loss was 22. Several other bombers were badly damaged, four of them so seriously that they were written off in landing accidents on returning to England.

During the last week of July 1943 the Eighth Air Force made five major sorties against 16 major targets. The longest mission was a 3057km (1900-mile) round trip to attack the German U-boat base at the Norwegian port of Trondheim. During seven days of operations 8th Bomber Command lost 88 aircraft, mostly Fortresses. This intensive phase began with the Trondheim attack on 24 July; the next day the target was the Blohm und Voss shipyards at Hamburg, obscured by a pall of smoke from the massive fires started by RAF Bomber Command the night before. At the same time other formations attacked the shipyards at Kiel and the Luftwaffe training school and airfield at Wustrow. Nineteen B-17s failed to return. On the 26th, the Fortresses struck at the Continental Gummiwerke AG, Hannover. They left the target in flames, with a massive mushroom of smoke rising to 6100m

(20,000ft). Sixteen bombers were shot down, and eight more were destroyed over Hamburg and other secondary targets.

THE 'BLOODY HUNDREDTH'

On 17 August 1943, the first anniversary of 8th Bomber Command's attack on Rouen in 1942, the Eighth Air Force mounted a maximum-effort strike on two nerve centres of the German aircraft industry, the Messerschmitt factory at Regensburg and the ball-bearing plants at Schweinfurt. What followed was the biggest air battle seen up to that time. An eye-witness to it was Lt Col Beirne Lay, Jr, flying as an observer on the Regensburg attack with a crew of the 100th Bombardment Group. Based at Thorpe Abbots in Suffolk, the 100th BG, which had been operational since 23 June 1943, was to suffer such appalling losses during its combat career that it became known as the 'Bloody Hundredth'.

'At 1017 hours, near Woensdrecht, I saw the first flak blossom out in our vicinity, light and inaccurate. A few minutes later, two FW 190s appeared at one o'clock and whizzed through the formation ahead of us in a frontal attack, nicking two B-17s in the wings and breaking away beneath us in half rolls. Smoke immediately trailed from both B-17s, but they held their stations. As the fighters passed us at a high rate of closure, the guns of our Groups went into action. The pungent smell of burnt powder filled our cockpit, and the B-17 trembled with the recoil of nose and ball gun turrets. I saw pieces fly off the wing of one of the fighters before they passed from view.'

'Here was early action. The members of the crew sensed trouble. There was something desperate about the way those two fighters came in fast right out of their climb without any preliminaries. Three minutes later the gunners reported fighters climbing up from all around the clock, singly and in pairs, both FW 190s and Me 109s. Every gun from every B-17 in our Group was firing, crisscrossing our patch of sky with tracers. Both sides got hurt in this clash, with two Fortresses from our low squadron and one from the Group ahead falling out of formation on fire with crews bailing out, and several fighters heading for the deck in flames with their pilots lingering behind under dirty yellow parachutes. I noticed an Me 110 sitting out of range on our right. He was to stay with us all the way to the target, apparently reporting our position to fresh squadrons waiting for us down the road. At the sight of all these fighters I had the distinct feeling of being trapped. The life expectancy of our Group suddenly seemed very short, since it appeared that the fighters were passing up the preceding Groups in order to take a cut at us.'

'Swinging their yellow noses round in a wide U-turn, a twelveship squadron of Me 109s came in from twelve o'clock in pairs and in fours, and the main event was on. A shining silver object sailed over our right wing. I recognized it as a main exit door. Seconds later, a dark object came hurtling through the formation, barely missing several props. It was a man, clasping his knees to his head, revolving like a diver in a triple somersault. I didn't see his 'chute open.'

'A B-17 turned gradually out of the formation to the right, maintaining altitude. In a split second, the B-17 completely disappeared in a brilliant explosion, from which the only remains were four small balls of fire, the fuel tanks, which were quickly consumed as they fell earthwards. Our airplane was endangered by falling debris. Emergency hatches, exit doors, prematurely opened parachutes, bodies, and assorted fragments of B-17s and Hun fighters breezed past us in the slipstream.'

'I watched two fighters explode not far beneath, disappearing in sheets of orange flame, B-17s dropping out on every state of distress, from engines shot out to control surfaces shot away, friendly and enemy parachutes floating down, and, on the green carpet far behind us, numerous funeral pyres of smoke from fallen fighters, marking our trail. The sight was fantastic: it surpassed fiction.'

'On we flew through the strewn wake of a desperate air battle, where disintegrating aircraft were commonplace and sixty 'chutes in the air at one time were hardly worth a sec-

Above: A B-17 of the 94th Bomb Group falls victim to bombs dropped by an aircraft in a higher formation during an attack on Berlin, its port horizontal stabiliser torn away.

ond look. I watched a B-17 turn slowly out to the right with its cockpit a mass of flames. The co-pilot crawled out of his window, held on with one hand, reached back for his 'chute, buckled it on, let go, and was whisked back into the horizontal stabilizer. I believe the impact killed him. His 'chute didn't open.'

THE ATTACKS CONTINUE

'Ten minutes, twenty minutes, thirty minutes, and still no letup in the attacks. The fighters queued up like a bread line and let us have it. Each second of time had a cannon shell in it. Our B-17 shook steadily with the fire of its .50s, and the air inside was heavy with smoke. It was cold in the cockpit, but when I looked across at the pilot I saw that sweat was pouring off his forehead and over his oxygen mask. He turned the controls over to me for a while. It was a blessed relief to concentrate on holding station in formation instead of watching those everlasting fighters boring in. It was possible to forget the fighters. Then the top turret gunner's muzzles would pound away a foot above my head, giving a realistic imitation of cannon shells exploding in the cockpit, while I gave an even better imitation of a man jumping six inches out of his seat.'

'A B-17 of the Group ahead, with its right Tokyo tanks on fire, dropped back to about 200 feet above our right wing and stayed there while seven of the crew successively bailed out. Four went out the bomb bay and executed delayed jumps, one bailed from the nose, opened his 'chute prematurely and nearly fouled the tail. Another went out the left waist gun opening, delaying his 'chute opening for a safe interval. The tail gunner jumped out of his hatch, apparently pulling the ripcord before he was clear of the ship. His 'chute opened instantaneously, barely missing the tail, and jerked him so hard that both his shoes came off. He hung limp in the harness, whereas the others had shown immediate signs of life after their 'chutes opened, shifting around in the harness. The B-17 then dropped back in a medium spiral

Below: The pilot, co-pilot, navigator, radio operator and bombardier of a B-17 study a map of the target area prior to departing on a mission. The final approach to a target required careful co-ordination.

and I did not see the pilots leave. I saw it just before it passed from view, several thousand feet below us, with its right wing a sheet of yellow flame.'

'After we had been under constant attack for a solid hour, it appeared certain that our Group was faced with annihilation. Seven of us had been shot down, the sky was still mottled with rising fighters, and it was only 1120 hours, with target-time still thirty-five minutes away. I doubt if a man in the Group visualized the possibility of our getting much further without one hundred per cent loss. I know that I had long since mentally accepted the fact of death, and that it was simply a question of the next second or the next minute. I learned firsthand that a man can resign himself to the certainty of death without becoming panicky. Our Group firepower was reduced thirty-three per cent; ammunition was running low. Our tail guns had to be replenished from another gun station. Gunners were becoming exhausted.'

'One B-17 dropped out of formation and put its wheels down while the crew bailed out. Three Me 109s circled it closely but held their fire, apparently ensuring that no-one stayed in the ship to try for home. Near the IP, at 1150 hours, one hour and a half after the first of at least 200 individual fighter attacks, the pressure eased off, although hostiles were still in the vicinity. We turned at the IP at 1154 hours with

fourteen B-17s left in the Group, two of which were badly crippled. They dropped out soon after bombing the target and headed for Switzerland.'

'Weather over the target, as on the entire trip, was ideal. Flak was negligible. The Group got its bombs away promptly on the leader. As we turned and headed for the Alps, I got a grim satisfaction out of seeing a rectangular column of smoke rising straight up from the Me 109 shops. The rest of the trip was a marked anticlimax. A few more fighters pecked at us on the way to the Alps. A town in the Brenner Pass tossed up a lone burst of futile flak. We circled over Lake Garda long enough to give the cripples a chance to rejoin the family, and we were on our way towards the Mediterranean in a gradual descent. The prospect of ditching as we approached North Africa, short of fuel, and the sight of other B-17s falling into the drink, seemed trivial matters after the vicious nightmare of the long trip across southern Germany. We felt the reaction of men who had not expected to see another sunset. At 1815 hours, with red lights showing on all the fuel tanks in my ship, the seven B-17s of the Group

Below: A Messerschmitt Bf110 (circled, right) turns in to make a stern attack on a B-17 (left) formation. The Bf110 was dangerous when armed with rockets, but was vulnerable to any escorting fighters.

which were still in formation circled over a North African airdrome and landed. Our crew was unscratched. Sole damage to the airplane: a bit of ventilation around the tail from flak and 20mm shells.'

'We slept on the hard ground under the wings of our B-17, but the good earth felt softer than a silk pillow.'

SCHWEINFURT

For the 8th Bomber Command the ordeal of 17 August 1943 was not yet over. In the early afternoon 229 Fortresses crossed the Dutch coast en route to bomb the ball-bearing factories at Schweinfurt. On this occasion determined fighter attacks began as soon as the formation reached German territory. The Gruppen attacked in pairs, one engaging the Allied fighter escort and the other the bombers. At times more than 300 German fighters were in the air, and fierce battles raged along the route to the target. In addition to cannon and machine guns, some of the fighters were armed with 21cm (8.25in) rockets. A direct hit by one of these was enough to tear a bomber apart, and several B-17s were lost by this means.

The fighter attacks intensified after the Americans' P-47 escort turned for home; 36 Fortresses were shot down, bringing 8th Bomber Command's total loss for the day to 60

Boeing B-17F-25-BO Flying Fortress

Specification:

Type: heavy bomber with crew 8 to 10
Powerplant: four 895kW (1200hp)
Wright R-1820-97 Cyclone
Performance: maximum speed
475km/h (295mph); initial climb rate
274m (900ft) per minute; service ceiling 10,975m (36,000ft); combat
radius with 2270kg (5000lb)
bombload 1287km (800 miles)
Weights: empty (typical) 15,422kg
(34,000lb); loaded (normal) 25,400kg
(56,000lb), (war overload from 1943)
32,660kg (72,000lb)

Dimensions: span 31.6m (103ft 9in);
length 22.8m (74ft 9in); height 5.85m
(19ft 2in); wing area 131.92m²
(1420 sq ft)
Armament: maximum bombload
4355kg (9600lb), later increased to
7983kg (17,600lb); defensive
firepower normally 11 guns of
12.7mm (0.5in) calibre and one of
7.62mm (0.3in) calibre

CHAPTER 5

Operations in Western Europe, 1944–45

With the advent of the Mustang to protect and escort the Fortresses all the way to the target and back again, aircraft losses fell, and consequently the damage caused to Germany's war effort rose immensely. At the same time production of the B-17 reached its wartime peak, and new aircraft were arriving in East Anglia in droves to join the fight against the Axis powers.

'First of all you must win the battle of the air. That must come before you start a single sea or land engagement. If you examine the conduct of my campaigns, you will find that we never fought a land battle until the air battle was won.'

So spoke Field Marshal Bernard Montgomery in December 1943, referring to the successful Allied campaigns of 1942–3 in North Africa. The initial object of these campaigns had been to defend the Suez Canal and the Anglo-Persian oilfields. When this had been achieved the goal was widened to include the elimination of the Axis forces in North Africa and the capture of the entire southern coast of the Mediterranean. By May 1943 the last pockets of Axis resistance in Tunisia had been wiped out, and General Erwin Rommel's once proud Afrika Korps had ceased to exist. Vast Allied land and air forces now stood idle in North Africa, and the question of their future employment became a matter of urgent priority.

With no prospect of launching an invasion of Occupied Europe from England in 1943, there remained two alternatives: either the forces in North Africa could be transferred to Burma and the Pacific to take part in the war against Japan, or they could follow up their African victory by invading Sicily and Italy. In the latter event the objective would be to eliminate Italy from the war and open the road for an Allied

Left: Escorted by P-51 Mustang fighters, B-17Gs head for Berlin. The long-range Mustang was able to escort the bombers all the way to their targets and back, engaging the German fighters.

Force, left the next day, having experienced problems with the hydraulic system, and narrowly escaped being shot down by Junkers Ju 88s over the Bay of Biscay.

The 97th Group was the first to deploy to North Africa, arriving at Maison Blanche in Algeria on 14 November, and it flew its first mission in the theatre – an attack on Bizerta harbour – two days later. The 301st BG went into action on 28 November.

At the beginning of 1943 both Groups were based at Biskra under the command of the newly-activated 5th Bombardment Wing, which was to exercise control over all B-17s in the Mediterranean Theatre. In March 1943 a third unit, the 99th BG (346th, 347th, 348th and 416th Squadrons) joined the Wing, and was followed at the end of April by the 2nd BG (20th, 49th, 96th and 429th Squadrons).

These four Groups were the only B-17 units assigned to the Twelfth Air Force. During the closing stages of the North African campaign they operated in a dual tactical and strategic role, supporting Allied land forces but also attacking harbours and shipping in and around North Africa and Italy. It was during this latter phase of the air campaign in North Africa that the vital lessons of joint command and control were thoroughly learned; the Twelfth Air Force was united with the RAF's Desert Air Force, and with the US Ninth Air Force – a tactical formation under the command of General Lewis H. Brereton – to eliminate the Axis forces in Tunisia. As the Allies converged on this last enemy bastion all their air power was combined as the Northwest African Air Forces under the command of General Carl Spaatz.

ATTACKS ON PANTELLERIA

In May 1943 B-17s of the 5th Wing joined other units in making heavy attacks on the island of Pantelleria, where Axis air and naval forces were in a good position to interfere with the forthcoming invasion of Sicily. After 25 days of almost continuous air bombardment, the Pantelleria garrison surrendered without a fight, and the way to Sicily was open.

Following the Allied invasion of Sicily and southern Italy in the summer of 1943, the four Twelfth Air Force B-17 Groups were assigned to the Fifteenth Air Force, which was activated on 1 November 1943. Henceforth, with occasional exceptions, the Fifteenth Air Force and its counterpart in England, the Eighth Air Force, would be committed to a single goal: the strategic air offensive against Germany.

At the beginning of 1944 the Americans established a new command structure for the conduct of strategic bombing in the European Theatre. At its apex were HQ US Strategic Air Forces under the command of General Carl Spaatz, while new commanders were appointed to the Air Forces that were to bear the brunt of the offensive. In England Lieutenant-General James H. Doolittle took over command of the Eighth Air Force from General Eaker, while the Fifteenth Air Force, now based in Italy, was commanded by Major-General Nathan F. Twining. These two forces, with 1000

Above: General Montgomery pictured aboard a B-17 shortly before the invasion of June 1944. Prior to this, the Fortresses joined other heavy bombers in attacking enemy communications in France.

advance into Austria and beyond, with the possibility of liberating Yugoslavia, Hungary and Czechoslovakia before the advancing Soviet armies did so.

This was the course that was chosen by the Allied leaders. It was an important decision, for the capture of Italian airfields would bring targets in southeast Germany within range of the heavy bombers of the US Fifteenth Air Force.

The first B-17s to serve in the Mediterranean Theatre were actually assigned to the US Twelfth Air Force, which was activated to support the Allied landings in North Africa in November 1942 (Operation Torch). Two Eighth Air Force Groups, the 97th and 301st, were committed to this operation, and six aircraft of the 97th Group's 340th Squadron were assigned to transport General Dwight D. Eisenhower and his staff from England to Gibraltar, from where the invasion would be directed. Five of the B-17s took off from Hurn aerodrome on 5 November 1942, a week before Operation Torch was due to begin; the sixth aircraft, carrying Major General James H. Doolittle, commander of the Twelfth Air

heavy bombers at their disposal, were assigned the task of carrying out Operation Argument – the destruction of the German aircraft industry, in particular those factories engaged in fighter production.

There was no doubt that the new bombing campaign would face fierce opposition, for the Luftwaffe's fighter strength had increased substantially during the winter months, when poor weather hampered Allied air operations, and the first raid of Operation Argument, on 11 January 1944, was proof enough that the Luftwaffe was capable of opposing the bombers with unprecedented ferocity. Undeterred, on 20 February the Eighth Air Force launched what was at that time the biggest ever daylight attack, when 941 bombers escorted by 700 fighters set out to bomb several key aircraft factories in central Germany between Leipzig and Braunschweig. The raid was heavily contested, but all the targets were hit by the bombers and 21 Fortresses were shot down, a figure that was considered an acceptable loss for such an operation.

Above: A B-17 formation seen at medium altitude. In general, the use of heavy bombers in the tactical role – as, for example, during the Normandy campaign – was not a success.

'BIG WEEK'

It was an encouraging start to the ten days of non-stop air onslaught that was to become known as 'Big Week'. On the night of 20/21 February, the American daylight success was followed up by a raid on Stuttgart, another centre of German aircraft production, by 600 Lancasters and Halifaxes of RAF Bomber Command. As the RAF crews returned, Fortresses and Liberators of the Eighth Air Force were being readied for another attack on the aircraft factories at Braunschweig. The following morning it was the turn of General Twining's Fifteenth Air Force in the Mediterranean, which had been heavily committed in support of the problem-hit Allied landings at Anzio. While a strong Fifteenth Air Force bomber force set out to attack the Messerschmitt aircraft factory at Regensburg from the south, the Eighth Air Force again left its

English bases to hit the factories in central Germany, as well as Gotha and Schweinfurt.

It was a bold attempt to crush the enemy defences between the jaws of a mighty pincer movement, but the mission was dogged by ill fortune from the start. To begin with, the Eighth's bases were covered by a dense cloud layer, and several bombers collided as they climbed up through it. The carefully laid plans for the assembly of the bomber force over eastern England were severely dislocated, and as a result two whole Bombardment Divisions, the 2nd and 3rd, were ordered to abort the mission and return. Only the 1st Division continued, and by this time the German warning radar stations, which had been monitoring the confused movements of the bombers as they tried to assemble, had fully alerted the Luftwaffe's fighter squadrons.

As the bombers crossed the German frontier they were savagely attacked by over 100 fighters of JG1 and JG2. The onslaught took the Americans by surprise; during previous attacks the Germans had concentrated their fighter defences in the immediate vicinity of the target, but this time they were attacking much farther to the west. They found the bombers escorted by only a handful of Thunderbolts; the

Above: A B-17 of the 483rd Bomb Group explodes over the target after being hit by flak during an attack on the marshalling yards at Nis, Yugoslavia, and goes down, taking its crew with it.

Mustangs were not due to rendezvous with the bombers until the latter were approaching the target area. What followed was a massacre. By the time the bomber stream reached the Harz Mountains the wrecks of 44 of their number lay scattered over a broad swathe of territory stretching back to the Rhineland. Only 99 out of the original force of 144 bombers that set out reached their primary targets, and only two of these targets were damaged. In the south the Fifteenth Air Force units successfully attacked the Messerschmitt factory at Regensburg, but they were strongly opposed by the fighters of the German 7th Air Division and 14 bombers were shot down.

DAIMLER-BENZ TARGETED

Bad weather brought a halt to strategic daylight operations for 24 hours. Then, on 24 February, 600 heavy bombers of the two Air Forces again set out for Germany. The Fifteenth Air Force's target was the Daimler-Benz aero-engine factory at

Styria, in eastern Austria, and once again the bombers were strongly opposed. Of the 87 Fortresses involved, 17 (20 per cent) failed to return. All ten bombers in the rear box were destroyed, most of them by salvoes of air-to-air rockets fired by Me 110s. Schweinfurt and Gotha, meanwhile, were heavily attacked by 477 Eighth Air Force bombers and both targets were badly hit, but the Americans lost another 44 aircraft. A third Eighth Air Force wave struck at Tutow, Kreising and Posen, which was bombed against minimal opposition. After dark Schweinfurt was again attacked by 700 Lancasters of RAF Bomber Command.

On 25 February favourable weather conditions extended over the whole of Germany, and the Strategic Air Forces launched over 800 bombers in a massive assault on the Messerschmitt factories at Regensburg and Augsburg from south and west. As two bomber streams approached Regensburg from these different points of the compass, the officer commanding 7th Air Division, Major-General Huth, was faced with a difficult decision. He did not have enough fighters to deal with both enemy forces. After some deliberation he decided to throw most of his available aircraft against the southern stream, consisting of 176 bombers. It was a wise choice; there was no fighter escort, and 33 Fortresses were shot down.

The bomber stream from the west, on the other hand, was considerably larger and was escorted by Mustangs. By this time three P-51 Groups were operational in Britain, and they soon began to make their presence felt. On this occasion comparatively few enemy fighters managed to break through; those that did, together with the flak, accounted for 31 out of a total force of 738 Fortresses and Liberators. The overall loss of 64 heavy bombers during the day's operations was not light, but the damage they inflicted on the aircraft factories was enormous. At Regensburg, the Messerschmitt works was practically levelled.

So ended 'Big Week', and judging by the reconnaissance photographs that showed aircraft factories all over Germany in ruins, it had been a success. The Germans took immediate steps to salvage what was left of the fighter production resources, but at first there was little hope. At Regensburg the Messerschmitt factory was such a wasteland of ruins that salvage work seemed impossible, and the German Air Ministry was on the point of authorising the erection of a factory on a different site when it received the first of a series of surprises. As workers dug into the rubble at Regensburg, they found that much of the factory's vital machinery was repairable and in some cases undamaged. The machine tools were housed in new, hastily-constructed workshops, and by the beginning of June the factory had regained its former level of output.

Below: Under the shadow of the wings of B-17s, a British Land Army worker gathers in the harvest in the late summer of 1944. The contrast between this scene and Europe's embattled skies was profound.

Protecting the B-17

As a counter to the German fighters waiting for them over the Channel, every aircraft on a raid formed up in a defensive box formation before setting out.

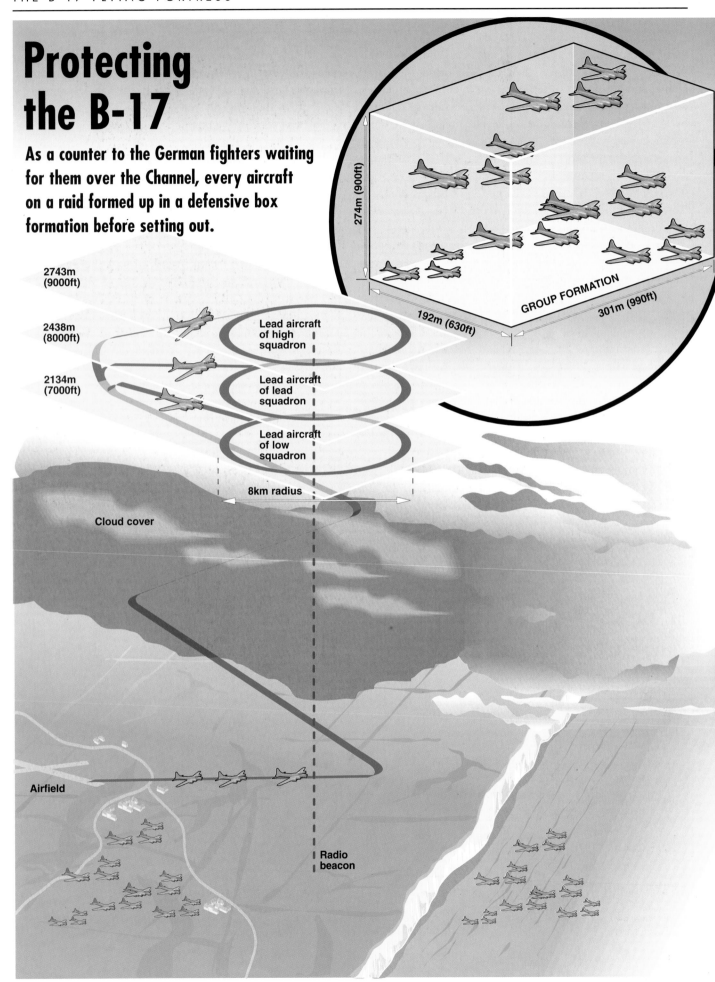

274m (900ft)

192m (630ft)

301m (990ft)

GROUP FORMATION

2743m (9000ft)

2438m (8000ft)

2134m (7000ft)

Lead aircraft of high squadron

Lead aircraft of lead squadron

Lead aircraft of low squadron

8km radius

Cloud cover

Airfield

Radio beacon

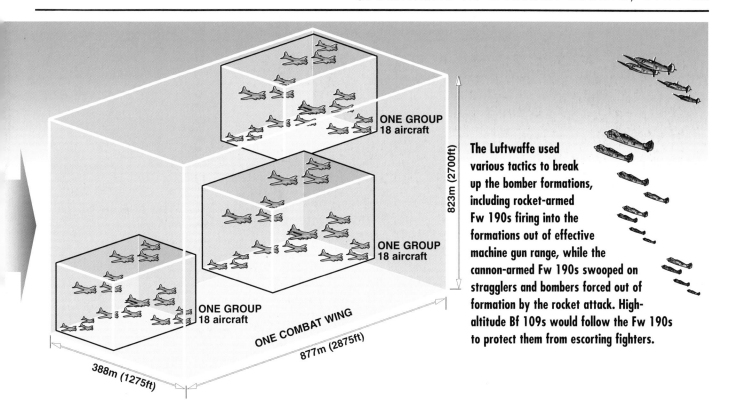

ONE GROUP
18 aircraft

ONE GROUP
18 aircraft

ONE GROUP
18 aircraft

823m (2700ft)

ONE COMBAT WING

877m (2875ft)

388m (1275ft)

The Luftwaffe used various tactics to break up the bomber formations, including rocket-armed Fw 190s firing into the formations out of effective machine gun range, while the cannon-armed Fw 190s swooped on stragglers and bombers forced out of formation by the rocket attack. High-altitude Bf 109s would follow the Fw 190s to protect them from escorting fighters.

Below: A chart showing the relative ranges of all the escort fighters used to protect the Flying Fortresses from German interception. At the very beginning of large-scale B-17 operations, the escorting RAF Spitfires did not have the range to protect the American bombers over Germany. Things improved as the war progressed, however, with the introduction of the longer-legged P-38 Lighting and P-47 Thunderbolt fighters. By 1944, the B-17s were escorted to the target and back by the excellent P-51 Mustang.

The Eighth Air Force used a variety of techniques to defend itself against the German fighters attempting to intercept any bomber force. Not only did the defensive armament of the B-17 improve, but so did the defensive tactics of the formation. By concentrating aircraft together in large numbers, the B-17s could bring an impressive amount of firepower to bear on any attacking aircraft. Throughout the latter part of the war the patterns within the box formations used by the Eighth Air Force changed several times as minor improvements in the formation were made, and as the Germans developed new techniques for attacking these 'Flying Fortresses'.

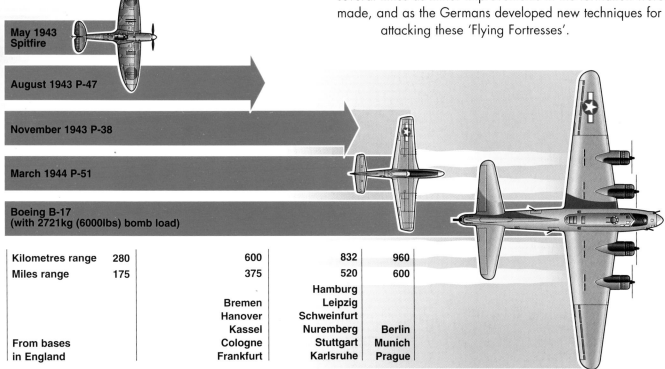

May 1943 Spitfire

August 1943 P-47

November 1943 P-38

March 1944 P-51

Boeing B-17 (with 2721kg (6000lbs) bomb load)

Kilometres range 280	600	832	960
Miles range 175	375	520	600
		Hamburg	
	Bremen	Leipzig	
	Hanover	Schweinfurt	
	Kassel	Nuremberg	Berlin
From bases	Cologne	Stuttgart	Munich
in England	Frankfurt	Karlsruhe	Prague

Left: While ground crew service the aircraft, another paints mission symbols on B-17G 'Nine O Nine' of the 333rd Bomb Squadron, 91st Bomb Group. This aircraft went on to complete 140 missions.

Above: Bombs falling on target during an attack on oil storage facilities at Regensburg, 18 December 1944. A raid on Regensburg a year earlier cost the Eighth Air Force some of its heaviest losses.

As for the Messerschmitt factory at Augsburg, it needed only two weeks of round-the-clock work before production was back to normal. At an aircraft factory near Leipzig 160 crated fighters were salvaged from the ruins; almost all were found to be repairable. Under the direction of Albert Speer, the minister of munitions and war production, factories were hastily dispersed to make it more difficult for the Allies to attempt another knockout blow.

LUFTWAFFE LOSSES

Although in the final analysis the 'Big Week' offensive made little difference to the output of single-seat fighters for the Luftwaffe, which reached the level of 2000 per month by the middle of 1944, the daylight offensive of January–April 1944 cost the Luftwaffe more than 1000 pilots, many of them experienced veterans. Although the claims of the Fortress and Liberator gunners were vastly inflated in the confusion of air battle, there was no escaping the fact that the Luftwaffe lost an average of 50 fighter pilots every time the Americans mounted a major raid. The Allied fighter escort, and particu-

larly the Mustangs, began to account for more enemy aircraft with every passing week.

On 6 March 1944 Mustangs appeared for the first time over Berlin and took part in one of the most bitterly contested air battles of the war. When it ended the Americans had lost 69 bombers – 15 of them belonging to the ill-fated 100th BG – and 11 fighters, but the Germans lost 80 aircraft, almost half the defending force. Another heavily escorted attack on Berlin by 590 bombers on 8 March, when several key factories were destroyed, cost the Americans 37 bombers and 17 fighters; but when 669 bombers again struck at the German capital on the 22nd they encountered almost no opposition. Twelve bombers were shot down, but all of them were victims of the flak.

During this period many long-range missions were flown by the Fifteenth Air Force's B-17s and B-24s to targets in the Balkans, the main strategic aim being to inflict as much damage as possible on that sector of the enemy's air power which could be brought to bear on the Italian war zone. Another aim was to delay the arrival of troop reinforcements

from the Balkans. To this end Sofia was heavily bombed six times in two months, the Bulgarian capital being the hub of the German-controlled supply system for all southeastern Europe. On 16 January 1944 Fortresses struck for the first time against the Messerschmitt aircraft factory at Klagenfurt, lying in the Carinthian Alps some 23km (14 miles) from the Yugoslav border, and on the 30th the Fifteenth Air Force attacked airfields in northeast Italy from which enemy bombers arriving from the Balkans refuelled before taking off to bomb the Allied concentrations in the Anzio and Nettuno bridgeheads.

THE FIGHTING FIFTEENTH

By this time the B-17s of the Fifteenth Air Force were concentrated on airfields around Foggia, in southern Italy, which brought them within comfortable range of many major targets which it had hitherto been impossible to attack. Two new groups arrived in the spring of 1944, bringing the strength of the 5th Wing up to six groups, all clustered around Foggia. The newcomers were the 463rd BG, which flew its first mission on 30 March 1944, and the 483rd BG, which began operations on 12 April.

For a time in March it had been touch and go for the Allied forces in Italy. Field Marshal Kesselring, the German commander, threw all his resources into repeated attacks on the

Above: Bombs shower from a formation of B-17s of the 545th Bomb Squadron, 384th Bomb Group. The 384th was one of the most decorated units – although over 1500 of its medals were posthumous.

Anzio beachhead, and after 36 hours of bitter fighting the Germans had begun to make substantial headway. At that point the Allies unleashed the whole weight of their strategic and tactical air power in the Mediterranean against the enemy; while fighter-bombers attacked enemy transport columns, B-17s and B-24s dropped 40,000 fragmentation bombs on troop concentrations and supply dumps in and around Cisterna, Carroceto and Campo Leone in a sustained and ferocious air onslaught that effectively halted the enemy counter-attacks.

Similar measures were applied, although with much less success, at Monte Cassino, where the Allied advance had ground to a halt against strong enemy defences. On 15 March 1944 the B-17 Groups joined other bomber units in dropping 1400 tons of bombs on the town, reducing it to rubble. But the bombing defeated its own object; the resulting devastation impeded the progress of Allied tanks, and the defenders – crack German paratroops, who had taken refuge in catacombs beneath the town and the ancient monastery during the air attack – were able to resist ferociously from strongpoints among the ruins.

CHAPTER 6

Foreign Fortresses

The B-17 was produced in such numbers that its use by other air forces comes as no surprise. As well as the Royal Air Force, the B-17 was used by the Luftwaffe, and after the war surplus Fortresses were used by the French Air Force, the Portuguese Air Force and, infamously, the new Israeli Air Force.

Although the B-17 is renowned for its operational service with the US Eighth and Fifteenth Air Forces in World War II, it actually began its combat career with the Royal Air Force, some months before America's entry into the war. In 1939, the US Government decided to offer 20 B-17C aircraft to the British Purchasing Commission, which was then actively seeking American equipment to expand the squadrons of the Royal Air Force. The Americans suggested that the aircraft, named Fortress Is by the British, should be used for training pending the release of more modern B-17 variants to the RAF, but the RAF had other ideas. The B-17 was a bomber, and as a bomber it would be used.

The first B-17C for the RAF, serial AN521, made the Atlantic crossing from Gander in Newfoundland to Burtonwood, Cheshire, on 14 April 1941, and was allocated to No 90 Squadron, RAF Bomber Command. Initially, the Fortresses were based at Bodney and West Raynham, Norfolk, and by mid-June 1941 the squadron had seven aircraft on strength. The seventh aircraft, AN522, had only been with the squadron a week when she was lost in an accident on 22 June, suffering catastrophic structural failure after her pilot lost control in violent turbulence at 10,065m (33,000 ft). The B-17 crashed near Catterick, Yorkshire, and there was only one survivor – a medical officer who had been on board to monitor the effects of high-altitude flying on the crew.

No 90 Squadron moved to Polebrook, Northamptonshire, towards the end of June 1941, and it was from there that the Fortresses flew their first operational mission on 8 July, when three aircraft were detailed to attack Wilhelmshaven at

Left: A Fortress GR IIA of 220 Squadron, RAF Coastal Command, taking off from Lagens airfield in the Azores. The squadron first deployed to Lagens in October 1943, and stayed there until the end of the war.

8235m (27,000ft), afterwards climbing to 9760m (32,000ft) to make their escape. Two aircraft bombed the target and the third, experiencing a severe oil loss, bombed Norderney instead. On 23 July three more Fortresses were detailed to bomb Berlin, but this mission had to be called off because of bad weather.

Meanwhile, the decision had been taken to use No 90 Squadron's Fortresses in high-level attacks on the German battlecruisers *Scharnhorst* and *Gneisenau* which, with the heavy cruiser *Prinz Eugen*, were lying in the French Channel ports of Brest and La Pallice. On 24 July 1941, three Fortresses consequently joined other RAF bombers in an attack on Brest, bombing from between 9150m (30,000ft) and 9760m (32,000ft), high above the rest of the force. The Fortress crews observed some of their 500kg (1100lb) bombs bursting on the torpedo station on the west side of the quay and also reported seeing only two or three enemy fighters, although the crews of the bombers attacking at lower level were heavily engaged. The outcome seemed to confirm the result of the Wilhelmshaven attack, when one Fortress crew had reported that their aircraft had been able to outclimb an enemy fighter attempting to intercept it at 9760m (32,000ft), and that other fighters had been forced to abandon the attack after suffering an apparent loss of control. Consequently, although the number of Fortresses in service with RAF Bomber Command was small, it was hoped that they might achieve a lot in the way of precision daylight attacks on the enemy.

RAID ON HAMBURG

The first Fortress mission after the Brest raid was flown on 26 July 1941, when two aircraft took off from Polebrook to bomb Hamburg. Both aircraft failed to bomb the primary target because of heavy thunderstorms; one returned to base with its bombs still on board (a usual procedure after an

Below: Boeing Fortress GR Mk II of No 220 Squadron in late 1942. This unit was based at Ballykelly, and was employed in the maritime patrol role for much of 1942 and 1943.

Above: A B-17C Fortress I of the RAF. After being withdrawn from the bomber role, some of these aircraft were used for long range maritime training pending the arrival of the Fortress II (a B-17F).

abortive mission, for the Fortresses' special 500kg (1100lb) bombs had to be obtained from the USA and were in short supply) and the other bombed Emden from a height of 9760m (32,000ft).

On 2 August a single Fortress made a successful attack on Kiel, dropping four 500kg (1100lb) bombs, and a second aircraft bombed Borkum. The latter aircraft was engaged by enemy fighters at 9760m (32,000ft) and suffered some damage before getting away; the crew had been unable to return fire because their machine guns were iced up. On 6 August the target was once again the German warships at Brest; one of the two Fortress crews that set out claimed to have hit one of the ships, but the other's bombs fell in the harbour because of aiming problems caused by a thick coat of ice on the bomb sight.

It was becoming apparent that high-altitude flying was attended by unexpected problems; apart from icing and engine trouble, another of No 90 Squadron's aircraft, AN534, had been lost on 26 July through structural failure following a loss of control during a high-altitude training flight. Like the previous one, this accident was caused by a combination of severe icing and high-level turbulence, the extent and vio-

Above: The Royal Air Force's B-17C Fortress I proved ineffective as a high-altitude daylight bomber, partly due to a lack of experience of high-altitude flying, and partly due to poor defensive armament.

lence of which at altitudes of over 9150m (30,000ft) had yet to be fully explored.

Four Fortresses took part in the Squadron's next mission, on 12 August. One bombed the Dutch airfield of de Kooy, another bombed Cologne from 10,370m (34,000ft), and a third attacked Emden from 10,065m (33,000ft). The fourth aircraft had engine trouble and was forced to abandon the mission. Four days later, on 16 August 1941, the Fortresses of No 90 Squadron suffered their first loss due to enemy action. Four aircraft were sent out, two to bomb Düsseldorf and two to attack Brest, but bad weather compelled the first pair to return with their bombs still on board. The other two dropped their bombs on Brest harbour from 10,675m (35,000ft) and 9760m (32,000ft) respectively, and immediately afterwards the lower aircraft was attacked by seven enemy fighters. The aircraft was badly damaged, but thanks to the height at which it was flying the pilot managed to reach the English coast, which was crossed at only 183m (600ft), too low for the crew to bale out. The pilot attempted to make a forced landing at Roborough, near Plymouth, but the aircraft crashed and caught fire, killing three of the crew. The enemy fighters had made a total of 26 attacks on the

Fortress, chasing it relentlessly until it was only 48km (30 miles) from the British coast.

FURTHER PROBLEMS

On 19 August an attempt to raid Düsseldorf by two Fortresses had to be abandoned when the guns of one aircraft froze and the other began to spin a contrail over the Dutch coast, giving away its position. High-altitude contrails were a continual source of concern to the Fortress crews, but there was nothing they could do about them except descend to a lower level, risking fighters and flak. A second attempt to bomb Düsseldorf on 21 August was also called off when two of the three aircraft taking part experienced severe icing and the other was forced to return with engine trouble. Another mission planned for 29 August was also unlucky; this time, one of the two aircraft detailed went unserviceable just before takeoff and the other aborted because of contrails.

A whole series of abortive operations followed. On 31 August one Fortress, bound for Hamburg, had to drop its load in the sea and return to base with oil trouble; a second aircraft was more fortunate and bombed Bremen, but because of heavy cloud the crew were unable to see the results. A third Fortress set off for Kiel, but returned with supercharger trouble. Bremen was attacked successfully by a lone Fortress on 2 September, but another aircraft bound for the same objective returned because of unfavourable cloud conditions and a third had to call off an attack on Duisburg when its intercom failed. The same aircraft experienced intercom trouble again on 4 September, causing the crew to abandon an attack on Hamburg. That same day two Fortresses set out for Hannover; one returned with engine failure and the other, experiencing contrail problems, bombed the docks at Rotterdam instead. This aircraft was attacked by a Me 109 at 9455m (31,000ft), but got away.

Meanwhile, on 6 August 1941, four Fortresses had been detached to Kinloss in northern Scotland for a mission against the battleship *Admiral Scheer*, which was lying in Oslo harbour. One aircraft returned to base with supercharger trouble; the other three reached Oslo but failed to locate the warship, aiming their bombs at the harbour installations instead. Four more Fortresses again set out for Oslo on 8 September. One of them, the last to take off, encountered ten-tenths cloud and returned to Kinloss. The other three, soon after crossing the Norwegian coast at 7930m (26,000ft), were intercepted by a strong force of Me 109s and two of the bombers were quickly destroyed. The third climbed rapidly to 10,675m (35,000ft) and turned for home, but some of the crew members began passing out through oxygen starvation and the pilot descended to 8845m (29,000ft). The fighters resumed their attacks, killing one gunner and wounding another. Bullets cut the wireless operator's oxygen tube and he collapsed.

Another burst of fire punctured a glycol tank, producing a long trail of white vapour which may have made the enemy fighter pilot think the Fortress was finished; he broke off the attack and disappeared. The Fortress flew on with one engine out of action and its controls severely damaged. Another engine failed during the return flight and the aircraft crashlanded at Kinloss, being totally wrecked.

DAYLIGHT RAIDS ABANDONED

Two more Fortress missions from Polebrook, with Cologne as the target, proved abortive. They were both carried out by the same aircraft on 15 and 16 September; on the first occasion the pilot turned back when he saw many enemy fighter contrails heading towards him, and on the second the mission was abandoned following a major power loss on two engines. On 20 September a Fortress dropped four 500kg (1100lb) bombs on Emden, but a further mission to the same target five days later was abandoned when the aircraft began to stream contrails at 8235m (27,000ft).

It was the last bombing mission carried out by the RAF's Fortresses in Europe. No 90 Squadron deployed its surviving aircraft to the Middle East in October, where they were absorbed and operated by a detachment of No 220 Squadron for two months.

Disastrous though it had been, the RAF's experience with the Fortress I had yielded some valuable lessons, not least of which was the need for improved defensive armament. It

Above: Boeing B-17C Fortress I in flight. Note the ventral gun blister, known as the 'bathtub'. This was replaced by a remote-controlled Bendix turret, which in turn was replaced by the familiar ball turret.

was also apparent that in future operations, B-17s would have to be sent out in tight formations and in considerable numbers, to make maximum use of overlapping patterns of defensive fire. There was also no doubt that the Sperry bombsight, with which the RAF's Fortresses were equipped, was greatly inferior to the American Norden for high-level precision bombing.

The home-based element of No 220 Squadron began conversion to Fortress Is at Nutts Corner in Northern Ireland in

January 1942 and used the aircraft on maritime reconnaissance duties until June, when it received the far more effective Fortress GR IIA (B17E). Its first operational sortie with the Fortress I was flown on 29 April 1942.

Shortly before it began to rearm with the Fortress GR IIA, No 220 Squadron moved to Ballykelly, which it shared with the very long range Consolidated Liberators of No 120 Squadron. This unit had received its first Liberator Is in June 1941 and had also been based previously at Nutts Corner. While the Liberators flew daily anti-submarine patrols in the Bay of Biscay area, usually refuelling at Predannack in Cornwall en route to their patrol areas, No 220 Squadron's Fortresses concentrated on convoy protection out to the

mid-Atlantic point, and also carried out air-sea rescue searches when called upon.

The second Coastal Command squadron to arm with the Fortress GR IIA was No 206, which exchanged its Lockheed Hudsons for the Fortress at Benbecula in August, and on 27 October 1942 it drew first blood for the RAF's maritime Fortresses when one of its aircraft attacked and sank the *U627* south of Ireland. On 15 January 1943 the squadron scored its second kill when a Fortress captained by Flying Officer Clark located and destroyed the *U337*, which had been operating in the area northeast of Newfoundland with the notorious 'Jaguar' U-boat pack; and on 3 February the *U265* became the squadron's third confirmed U-boat victim when it was attacked by a Fortress escorting Convoy SC118 in the North Atlantic.

For No 220 Squadron, still at Ballykelly, the long hours of fruitless Atlantic patrolling ended in February 1943. On the 6th, the *U456*, transmitting the position of SC118 to bring other U-boats to the scene, was attacked and heavily bombed by an escorting Fortress, which succeeded in driving off this particular boat and several others in the vicinity. On the following day, another 220 Squadron Fortress attacked and sank the *U624*, bringing the squadron its first confirmed victory, and on 7 March, having moved to the neighbouring airfield of Aldergrove in the meantime, No 220 claimed its second submarine victim, the *U633*, which was bombed and sunk south of Iceland.

FURTHER SUCCESS

A few days later the pendulum again swung in favour of No 206 Squadron. On 25 March a squadron aircraft bombed and sank the *U469*, operating as part of the 'Seeteufel' (Sea Devil) U-boat group against Convoy SC123 to the south of Iceland, and two days later another 206 Squadron crew caught and destroyed the *U169*, belonging to the same group. On 24 April the Squadron destroyed its sixth enemy submarine, sinking the *U710*, which was attempting to close with Convoy HX234 from Halifax, Nova Scotia. Anti-submarine operations were not without their attendant dangers; on 12 March 1944, for example, a 206 Squadron Fortress was shot down by the *U311*, which it was attempting to attack on the surface. The Squadron had its revenge the next day, however, when one of its Fortresses helped to hunt down the *U575*, which was sunk by escort vessels.

In the meantime, No 220 Squadron had enjoyed further success. Now based in the Azores, one of its Fortresses accounted for the *U707* in November 1943, but in the following month it lost an aircraft to the gunfire of the *U764*

Below: *Wulf Hound*, a B-17F-27-BO (41-24585 PU∗B) of the 303rd Bomb Group, was the first B-17 to fall intact into enemy hands, having made an emergency landing in Holland on 12 December 1942.

and another was shot down on 6 January 1944 by the *U270*, the submarine also being damaged by its victim. No 220 Squadron claimed its last U-boat on 26 September 1944, sinking the *U871* northwest of the Azores. By that time the Squadron was operating with B-17Gs, known as Fortress IIIs in Coastal Command service.

No 59 Squadron, based at Aldergrove, also operated Fortress IIs for a brief period from January–March 1943 before converting to Liberators, and No 251 Squadron, based on Iceland for air–sea rescue duties, converted to Fortress IIs in March 1945.

FORTRESSES OF THE LUFTWAFFE

It is an extraordinary fact that, after the RAF, the biggest user of the B-17 was the Luftwaffe. With large numbers of Fortresses operating over occupied Europe, it was inevitable that some should fall into enemy hands either intact or in a repairable condition. Seven are known to have been operated by the Luftwaffe in total; the first was a 303rd BG B-17F named *Wulf Hound* (41-24585), which was badly damaged during an attack on the marshalling yards at Rouen on 12 December 1942, intercepted by a Messerschmitt 110, and forced to land at Leeuwarden in occupied Holland. After repair, the bomber was given German insignia and flown to the Luftwaffe test centre at Rechlin, where German engineers spent the next three months analysing the Fortress' systems and compiling data in readiness for the first of a series of test flights. On 17 March 1943 *Wulf Hound* made her first flight in German hands, and after several more test sorties the aircraft made a tour of the Luftwaffe fighter groups in France and Germany to help develop new fighter tactics to use against the B-17.

Back at Rechlin, *Wulf Hound* was used to conduct further trials, including glider towing, until September 1943, when she was assigned to KG200 – the Luftwaffe's special operations unit – at Rangsdorf. She was repainted in night camouflage for clandestine missions, but no record of her operational service with KG200 exists, and the eventual fate of *Wulf Hound* is unknown.

Above: *Wulf Hound* was the first of several Flying Fortresses to be tested by the Luftwaffe. Some B-17s were impressed into operational service with KG200, the Luftwaffe's clandestine special duties unit.

Another Fortress assigned to KG200 was B-17F *Down and Go!* (4230146 of the 94th BG), which had engine problems during an attack on Warnemunde on 29 July 1943, tried to reach neutral Sweden, but had to make a belly landing in a field some six miles from Copenhagen. After major repairs, *Down and Go!* was allocated to a unit within KG200 known as Kommando Olga, which, commanded by Major Peter Stahl, was tasked with dropping agents, saboteurs and supplies behind Allied lines. Kommando Olga shared its base at Stuttgart-Echterdingen with Transportgeschwader 30 (TG30), which was equipped with Heinkel He 111s and had the job of delivering mail and supplies to German garrisons in western Europe – for example in the Channel Islands – which had been isolated by the Allied invasion of June 1944.

On the night of 9/10 February 1945, the crew of *Down and Go!* was briefed for a top-secret mission that involved the delivery by parachute of ten agents and officials of the Vichy French Government who had actively collaborated with the Germans to a drop zone on the Franco–Spanish border, the first stage of an escape route out of Europe. At 2200, with 19 crew and passengers on board, *Down and Go!* took off from Stuttgart and began to climb, but at about 91m (300ft) the Fortress exploded without warning and plunged to earth in flames, killing all on board except two gunners, who were thrown clear and survived.

FLAK DANCER

Another Fortress used by the Germans was *Flak Dancer*, a B-17F (42-30048) which made a belly landing at Laon airfield on 26 June 1943. The last Fortress to be captured in 1943 was *Miss Nonalee II*, a 385th Bomb Group B-17F (42-30336), which also tried to reach Swedish territory after suffering engine problems on 9 October 1943, but only made it as far as a meadow at Norholm Mark, near Varde in Denmark. German engineers prepared a temporary grass strip and,

after being stripped of all unnecessary equipment to reduce weight, the bomber took off on three engines and was flown to Esbjerg, where her equipment was refitted before the aircraft went on to Rechlin. From there, like *Wulf Hound*, she was sent on a tour of German fighter bases; her last recorded detachment was to Leipzig-Brandis in December 1944. Her fate after that remains unknown.

The first B-17G to be captured intact was an unnamed aircraft (42-38017 XR*O) of the 100th Bombardment Group, which landed at Schleswig on 3 March 1944. Five days later *Phyllis Marie*, a B-17F (42-30713) fell into enemy hands at Werben, and on 9 April 1944 a B-17G (42-39974) of the 731st Squadron, 452nd Bomb Group, was forced down at Vaerlose airfield, Denmark, and subsequently shipped to Rechlin.

Four B-17s in total are believed to have been operated by KG200. Clandestine operations took crews as far afield as Transjordan, Greece, the Soviet Union and Ireland; until KG200 received a few Junkers Ju 290 transports, the B-17 was the only available aircraft with enough range and load-carrying capacity to undertake long-range missions of this kind. The last weeks of the war found three of KG200's B-17s (and a captured B-24) based at Wackersleben, in eastern Germany, and in April arrangements were made to evacuate the surviving aircraft to Fürstenfeldbruck, in the west. The three B-17s and the B-24 took off on 6 April, but only one of the B-17s reached its destination. One crashed into a mountainside in the Thuringer Wald; the other was shot down by friendly fire at Altenburg. Which of the captured B-17s these aircraft were, unfortunately, remains a mystery.

Germany's Axis partner, Japan, also flew a small number of B-17s, captured during the early Japanese conquests in the

Pacific and Netherlands East Indies. After being evaluated, these aircraft were used exclusively for fighter affiliation. Their eventual fate is unknown.

ISRAELI B-17S

In 1948, the infant state of Israel acquired three war-surplus B-17Gs and, curcumventing a US arms embargo, had them ferried to a clandestine base in Czechoslovakia via Panama and Portugal. They arrived during the last week of June and were overhauled by a detachment of Jewish personnel under the direction of a former B-17 pilot named Ray Kurtz. On 7 July, Kurtz received a signal from Tel Aviv instructing him to prepare the bombers for an attack on Cairo, Gaza and El Arish as a reprisal for Egyptian air raids on Israel. The mission was ordered for 15 July, each aircraft carrying a maximum

Below: A B-17G of the Israeli Air Force in 1948. Note the Mickey Mouse motif on the tail fin. All defensive armament has been removed with the exception of the tail guns.

Above: Flying Fortresses in Israeli markings. Three aircraft reached Israel by a circuitous route in 1948 and were used operationally in Israel's war of 1948–49 against the surrounding Arab states.

load of fuel and a minimum bomb load of 228kg (500lb) bombs. The story of the raid was a saga in itself.

The Israeli Air Force's three B-17Gs were used operationally in the 1948–49 War of Independence, in both bomber and transport roles, and were still in service during the Sinai campaign of 1956, although they were withdrawn shortly afterwards. The aircraft were not fitted with chin, dorsal or ventral guns and bore a colour scheme of sand yellow, green and olive green over neutral grey, on which was superimposed the Israeli national insignia. One of the aircraft carried a bomb-wielding Mickey Mouse on its tail fin.

INTERNED FORTRESSES

From August 1943, when the Eighth Air Force began its deep penetration attacks into enemy territory, B-17s and B-24s

FOREIGN FORTRESSES

THE ATTACK ON EGYPT

Trouble hit Kurtz's aircraft almost immediately. During the run-up before take-off, two amplifiers burnt out, the propeller governor of number one engine froze at 2400 rpm, the manifold pressure of number two engine refused to rise above 18 inches and the artificial horizon ceased to function. Kurtz would have been entirely justified in aborting the mission, but he did not. At 1000 local time the last of the three aircraft took off and climbed to 10,000 feet. The B-17s flew southwards in loose formation, the pilots juggling with the throttles to maintain the most economical cruise and to nurse engines that were already beginning to overheat. Kurtz was running into further mechanical difficulties; several more instruments had become inoperative and the port inner engine was running erratically, its oil pressure fluctuating.

Then they flew into bad weather and severe turbulence over Austria, skirting the eastern fringe of the Alps, and the three aircraft split up to reduce the risk of collision. With some of the Fortresses' most vital instruments out of action, flying through the murk was a nightmare. For 30 minutes Kurtz fought to hold the aircraft steady as it was subjected to severe turbulence. By the time it emerged into clearer skies, the pilot was almost exhausted and the other members of the crew were feeling ill and wretched; some of them had been violently airsick.

The Fortresses joined up again over the coast of Yugoslavia, were subjected to some brief and inaccurate anti-aircraft fire over Albania, and flew on towards Crete, where they split up and headed for their individual targets. Cairo was Ray Kurtz's objective. Halfway across the Mediterranean he put the B-17 into a steady climb, crossing the North African coast at 7625m (25,000ft). With every passing minute, Kurtz was finding it harder to keep the aircraft on a straight course; he was feeling light-headed, and some of the other eight crew members were experiencing the same symptoms.

Suddenly, the navigator collapsed over his chart table, and at last Kurtz realized what the trouble was. In Czechoslovakia, the aircraft had been fitted with cylinders containing welder's oxygen, which was totally unsuitable for breathing at altitude. Kurtz ordered all the crew members to turn their oxygen on to 'emergency', and after a while the situation eased a little.

One of the crewmen worst affected was Johnnie Adir, the bombardier. He had rigged up a makeshift bomb sight salvaged from a wrecked German aircraft, and no one else had any idea how to use it. If Adir passed out, the mission would fail. Kurtz ordered him to get as much rest as possible.

Kurtz had no difficulty in locating the Egyptian capital. For one thing, the B-17's radio equipment was tuned in to a homing beacon beaming out a steady signal from the RAF base at Fayid, in the Canal Zone; all he had to do was follow it and it would take him right over the top of Cairo. For another thing, Cairo itself was brightly lit. As they approached, Johnnie Adir, somewhat recovered, clambered into his position in the bomber's nose. His target was Cairo's main airport, which he had no difficuly in locating.

As soon as the bombing run was completed and the two bombs released, Kurtz turned back towards the coast and began a descent, the crew gradually recovering as the bomber lost altitude. The Fortress crossed the coast of near Port Said, and at 2245, local time, it landed at Ekron airfield near Tel Aviv. The two other B-17s also landed safely, the crews reporting successful attacks on their targets. In fact, the damage caused was negligible, but the three attacks did much to boost the morale of the Israeli people. (From: *The Israeli Air Force Story* by Robert Jackson, Tandem Books 1972)

frequently entered Swiss air space to avoid pursuing Luftwaffe fighters. Many of the B-17s were crippled and could barely keep aloft, and the Swiss fighter pilots (mainly flying early Messerschmitt 109s) escorted the damaged aircraft to the nearest airfield. Usually, the bombers were escorted by four fighters, two of them guiding the bomber to the airfield and the other two bringing up the rear to head off the bomber should its crew decide that internment was not for them. Twenty B-17s landed in Switzerland; all were meticulously examined before being scrapped.

OTHER FOREIGN FORTRESSES

Among the foreign air arms to use the Flying Fortress in the post-war years was Portugal, which used five SB-17Gs for search and rescue betweeen 1947 and 1960. B-17Gs were transferred to the Dominican Air Force, while SB-17Gs served with the Brazilian Air Force's 6th Grupo de Aviacao. The Free French Air Force used a small number of B-17Fs in Indo-China during the closing stages of the war against Japan, and also used modified B-17Gs in the transport and survey roles. Thirteen B-17Gs in all were acquired between 1947 and

81

Above: Seven B-17s (from the 68 which were interned in Sweden) were converted into 14-seat airliners by AB Aerotransport. TWA converted a B-17 for use as an executive transport.

1955, all from surplus USAAF or US Government sources, and one of the B-17Fs already in French Air Force service was retained for spares.

IGN FORTRESSES

The aircraft were operated by the *Institut Geographique National* (IGN), whose main base was at Creil, near Paris, and the last of them, F-BEEA, continued to serve until the late 1980s. This Fortress, named Chateau de Verneuil, previously

carried the USAAF serial 44-85643. Some of the aircraft had interesting histories. One of them, F-BGSH, was previously 42-32076 LL-E *Shoo Shoo Baby* of the 401st BS, 91st BG, which was based at Bassingbourn. On 29 May 1944 the aircraft was compelled to make an emergency landing in Sweden, where it was interned and allocated the civil registration SE-BAP. (Seven of the 68 B-17s in total that landed in Sweden during the war entered service – after some modification – as 14-seat airliners with AB Aerotransport.)

In November 1945 the aircraft was acquired by Denmark as OY-DFA *Store Bjorn*, and in April 1948 it was impressed by the Royal Danish Air Force for aerial survey work in Greenland; based at Kastrup, the aircraft was assigned to

No 721 Squadron and served in the survey role until 1954, before being purchased by IGN. F-BGSH made its last flight on 15 July 1961. In February 1972 a USAF C-5A Galaxy transport flew it from Rhein-Main AB, Germany, to Dover AFB, Delaware, for restoration.

LOST B-17S

Two of IGN's B-17s came to grief during their operational careers. On 11 March 1949 F-BEEB crashed at Yaounde, Cameroun, with the loss of five crew, and F-BDAT crashed at Niamey, Niger, on 12 December 1950. Other IGN Fortresses ended their days on the scrapheap; F-BDRR and F-BEED were both scrapped in 1962, while F-BGOE met a similar fate in 1970 and F-BGSQ in 1972. Something of a mystery surrounds F-BGOE; it was purchased from the Shah of Iran in 1952, but no record exists of its Iranian service. The B-17F (42-30177), which had served with the USAAF 388th BG and subsequently with the Free French as *Bir Hakeim*, was also scrapped in 1973.

PRESERVED FORTRESSES

The remainder, more fortunately, were earmarked for preservation. F-BDRS went to the Imperial War Museum at Duxford in May 1975 for restoration as *Mary Alice* of the 401st BG, while F-BEEC, which saw service in South Africa as ZS-EEC from August 1965 to August 1966, went to Warbirds of Great Britain as G-FORT in June 1984. F-BGSO went to the Musee de l'Air in September 1976, and F-BGSP was restored to flying condition as the 381st BG's *Lucky Lady*. This aircraft, originally 44846, saw brief service with the 511th BS of the 351st Bomb Group, and in 1998, after being overhauled by Air France Industries at Orly, she was rolled out in her wartime colours, bearing the new name *Pink Lady*.

Finally, F-BGSR was sold off to Ted White/Euroworld in 1975. Registered as G-BEDF, she can now be seen restored to her former glory as the famous Duxford-based *Sally B*.

Below: B-17F-115 had formerly been known as *Veni Vidi Vici* of the 388th Bomb Group, based at Knettishall. On 29 February 1944 it landed in Sweden: eight months later it emerged as an airliner.

CHAPTER 7

Special Fortresses, Special Missions

So good was the basic B-17 airframe, that it lent itself to a number of conversions and adaptations throughout its service life, and these variants were to soldier on for some time after their bomber siblings had been retired from duty.

Early in 1941, the USAAC carried out a series of experiments with primitive glider bombs at Wright Field, Dayton, Ohio, to study the feasibility of developing an operational weapon that could be released outside the range of heavy flak defences and penetrate through to the target under radio guidance from a parent aircraft. Development of one project, the Aeronca GB-1, continued into 1942, research being undertaken partly in industry and partly at the Air Technical Service Command and the Air Proving Ground at Wright Field.

The missile that emerged was a standard 907kg (2000lb) GP bomb fitted with 12ft (3.66m) wooden wings and twin fins and tailplane supported by twin booms. At the rear of the bomb was the radio receiver and control servo, which biassed a simple Hammond autopilot to keep the bomb on the right trajectory. As designed, the GB-1 would be aimed at the target like any other bomb, with corrections made for wind drift and trajectory by the bombardier before release, which would occur at 32km (20 miles) from the target at an altitude of 4572m (15,000ft).

The concept was tested during the spring and summer of 1943 with a B-17E trials aircraft, and it was found that a Fortress could easily carry two of the new weapons, attached directly to release stations between the wing root and the inboard engine nacelles. Plans were made to train a number of crews in GB-1 launch procedures, and to convert B-17s to carry the missiles.

By the summer of 1943, with Eighth Air Force losses over Germany rising to alarming proportions, the project had taken on a considerable sense of urgency. Accordingly, 40 GB-1 equipped B-17s and their crews were deployed to England, arriving on 29 September 1943 and being assigned to the 41st Bomb Wing of the Eighth Air Force's 3rd

Left: A PB-1G Fortress of the United States Coast Guard carrying a moulded plywood lifeboat. This Fortress variant continued to serve in the air-sea rescue role for some years post-World War II.

Bombardment Division. The B-17s were allocated to three bomb groups, the 303rd, 379th and 384th, at Kimbolton, Grafton Underwood and Molesworth.

However, because of the losses suffered by the Eighth Air Force during the attacks on Regensburg and Schweinfurt in August and early October, the newly arrived bombers were converted for normal operations and their crews given regular assignments. In addition, the prevailing European weather was too poor to permit the use of the GB-1, which needed clear sighting conditions. The GB-1 concept was therefore shelved throughout the winter of 1943–4, and it was not until May 1944 that the Eighth Air Force had an opportunity to prove the weapon under combat conditions.

On 28 May 1944, 60 B-17s from the three 41st Wing bomb groups took off from their respective bases and headed for the big Eifeltor marshalling yards at Cologne. The Fortresses approached the target area in a spread-out formation so that each missile would have a clear path from the release point. The bombardiers had no difficulty in identifying the target in the clear weather, and 54 bombers released a total of 108 GB-1s. Looking rather like a swarm of insects, the missiles reached a speed of about 644km/h (400mph) as they headed for the target area, and it was now that the GB-1's shortcomings became apparent. Only a few of the bombs landed in the target area; some drifted badly off track, others devel-

oped too steep an angle of glide and exploded short, or overshot the target altogether. Damage to the marshalling yards was negligible; the only plus point for the mission was that all the parent B-17s returned to base.

About 1000 GB-1s and a developed version, the TV-guided GB-4, were subsequently aimed at targets in Germany, including the S-boat pens at Le Havre and La Pallice early in 1945, but results never improved appreciably. GB-4 trials were carried out by the 388th BG at Fersfield, in Suffolk, under the code-name of Operation Batty.

PROJECT APHRODITE

It was at Fersfield, too, that the Eighth Air Force conducted its evaluation of the Project Aphrodite concept, which envisaged the use of time-expired bombers – mostly B-17s and B-24s – packed with explosive and radio-guided to enemy targets. The technique was for the explosive drone, designated BQ-17, to be taken off manually and piloted towards the British coast. A second crew member, an electronics specialist, would set the autopilot and radio receiver and the two crew would then bale out, an accompanying 'mother ship'

then taking over control and guiding the drone to the target area. The principal object was to inflict damage on the V-1 launching sites that were detected by air reconnaissance in the Pas de Calais area in the summer of 1944.

The first operation was flown on 4 August 1944, when two BQ-17 drones set off to make an attack on the V-1 sites. One of these aircraft stalled and dived into the ground soon after remote control was assumed, killing one of the crew; the other was steered to the target area, but refused to dive on command. It was hit by flak and exploded. The crew of a third BQ-17, launched later in the day, baled out safely, but the drone overflew its target and exploded harmlessly. A fourth BQ-17 undershot its objective, one of its crew having been seriously injured as he baled out.

Another mission was scheduled for 6 August. This time only two BQ-17s were involved, code-named Franklin Yellow and Franklin White. The former carried nine tons of Torpex, the latter 160 incendiary bombs and 3774 litres (830 gallons) of napalm. This mission also ended in fiasco when the crew of the mother ship lost control of the Franklin Yellow BQ-17 just after its crew had baled out; in fact they lost sight of it

Above: Jewish agents at Anske-Bistortza airstrip waiting to be dropped into Hungary. A B-17 used for clandestine operations is parked in the background, apparently wearing Russian markings.

altogether, and when they found it again after a frantic search, it was flying in circles over the town of Ipswich. They managed to re-establish enough control over the aircraft to crash the drone in the sea off the Suffolk coast. The Franklin White sortie was also unsuccessful.

After this, tentative plans were made to use the BQ-17s against shipping targets and harbour installations, and on 11 September 1944 a mission was laid on against the U-boat pens at Heligoland. A BQ-17F (230180) was loaded with 8346kg (18,425lb) of torpex and steered across the North Sea, only to be shot down into the sea about 320m (1050ft) from its target. Again, one of the drone's crew members was killed on baling out.

In another mission, two BQ-17s were despatched against an oil refinery at Henningstadt; one overshot the target by about 305m (1000ft), while contact with the other was lost after it was accidentally overtaken by the parent aircraft. On

15 October 1944 two more BQ-17s were despatched against installations on Heligoland; one was destroyed by AA fire short of the target, but the other exploded on its objective and caused substantial damage. On 5 December an abortive mission was flown by two drones against Herford, and after that Project Aphrodite was abandoned.

COUNTERMEASURES

On 8 November 1943 the RAF established a special bomber support force, No 100 Group, under the command of Air Vice-Marshal E.B. Addison. Its primary functions were to give direct support to Bomber Command by attacking enemy night-fighters, and to employ airborne and ground RCM to jam the German radio navigational aids, radar systems and wireless signals.

Several problems were experienced in the creation of No 100 Group's radio countermeasures force. The first lay in the choice of a suitable aircraft, which had to be big enough to carry the necessary equipment and able to fly fast and high enough to stand a chance of avoiding night-fighters. The aircraft selected eventually was the Boeing B-17 Flying Fortress, which was considered to meet all the requirements. Fourteen B-17Fs were obtained, and necessary modifications were carried out early in 1944 by the Scottish Aviation Company at Prestwick. These included the replacement of the Fortress's chin turret by a H_2S blister, the provision of mufflers to screen the exhaust flames and the fitting of the jamming devices in the bomb bay. The aircraft began operations with No 214 Squadron in June 1944. In addition, B-17s of the 803rd Squadron, United States Strategic Air Forces, were also equipped for the jamming role, and this unit was placed under the operational control of No 100 Group.

The RCM equipment carried by these aircraft was called Jostle and Piperack. The first, a high-powered communications jammer, emitted a high-pitched wail and could effectively jam any frequency used by the German fighter controllers; the second, developed from an American RCM kit called Dina, covered the 90–110 mc/s frequency used by the German AI radars. A third squadron, No 223, which was

equipped with Liberators and Fortresses and which began operations in September 1944, was also equipped with these devices. Other RCM operations, which did not require fast, high-flying aircraft since they were usually conducted clear of enemy territory, were flown by the Stirlings of No 199 Squadron and the Halifaxes of No 171, joined at the end of 1944 by the Halifaxes of No 642 Squadron. Among other devices, these aircraft were equipped with Mandrel, a radar jammer developed at the Wembley laboratories of the General Electric Company. It operated in the 120–130 mc/s band, and two aircraft per squadron were to be fitted with it. Its object was to reduce the range at which the German Freya radar sets could identify and plot incoming bombers from 160 to about 40km (100 to 25 miles).

In their finalised form, the tactics used by No 100 Group's RCM force were as follows. Mandrel-equipped aircraft, employed mainly to provide a screen for the main bomber force, would operate in pairs with 14 miles between them, forming a line positioned some 130km (80 miles) from enemy territory. With their Mandrels switched on, the orbiting aircraft formed an effective electronic curtain through which the enemy search radars were unable to penetrate. The B-17s equipped with Jostle and Piperack, on the other hand, flew 1220m (4000 feet) above the bomber stream at intervals of 16km (10 miles), providing an electronic umbrella to disrupt the German AI radar and voice communications.

All B-17s operating with No 100 Group were painted black overall. Since the ball turret was retained, the H_2S radar blister, normally housed amidships in other types, was placed under the nose.

FAILED FIGHTER FORTRESS: THE YB-40

In November 1942, following preliminary studies and USAAF recommendations, the Vega Aircraft Corporation – a division of Lockheed – was given the task of developing a so-called

Below: Boeing Fortress III of No 214 Squadron. This unit operated in the electronic countermeasures role with No 100 Group, specialising in jamming enemy radar and communications.

'destroyer escort plane', a heavily armed B-17 which would attach itself to Fortress bomber formations and lend substantial weight to their defensive firepower. Its prototype was the second B-17F, 41-24341, which after modification was designated XB-40.

The XB-40 had an armament of 14 0.50in calibre machine guns, installed in pairs in the following positions: Bendix chin turret with 400 rounds per gun, Sperry model 250CE4 mid upper turret with 400 rounds per gun, Briggs lower ball turret with 600 rounds per gun, tail position with 550 rounds per gun, and in both waist positions with 300 rounds per gun. In addition to the total of 5900 rounds positioned with the guns themselves, provision was made for 6500 rounds of reserve ammunition, most of it stored in the radio operator's compartment.

As the B-40 was likely to be exposed in its defensive position on the flanks of a bomber formation, extra armour was provided for the crew and engines. These additions to the standard B17F airframe not only increased the weight to 28,673kg (63,295lb) and reduced the maximum speed to around 466km/h (290mph) at 9150m (30,000ft); they also

Below: Personnel inspecting the wreck of a crash-landed Coast Guard PB-1G. The PB-1G was also used for photo-mapping, for which role it was fitted with a nine-lens camera costing $1,500,000.

badly affected the handling characteristics of what was normally a pleasant and stable aircraft.

By February 1943 Vega had completed the first of an initial batch of 13 aircraft, intended for operational evaluation and designated YB-40-VE. In April 1943 the Eighth Air Force reactivated its oldest bomber group, the 92nd, and in May 12 YB-40s were flown into its base at Alconbury, in Huntingdonshire. After several practice flights, the first operational mission – a sortie to St Nazaire – was flown on 29 May, and served only to confirm what the trial flights had already revealed; that the heavy YB-40 found great difficulty in keeping station with the ordinary B-17s, and even more difficulty in keeping pace with them once they had dropped their bombloads.

After this first mission, the YB-40s were taken off operations while modifications were made to the tail and waist gun feeds. Also, two extra 0.50in guns were installed in nose windows for the use of the navigator, making a total of sixteen and increasing the weight to 28,765kg (63,500lb) and further reducing the maximum speed at altitude to 458km/h (285mph). By way of comparison, the all-up weight of a standard B-17F was 24,915kg (55,000lb) and maximum speed was 503km/h (313mph).

On 22 June 1943 all 11 serviceable YB-40s were despatched on an escort mission to Huls, one flight being

assigned to each of the four most vulnerable bomber groups on the mission. The growing feeling that the YB-40 might be unable to defend itself, let alone the bombers it was escorting, was strengthened when the only aircraft lost on this mission was a YB-40, shot down by fighters over Holland.

Operations by the YB-40s continued for a few more weeks, but their frequency gradually diminished as more aircraft were lost or became unserviceable. In the end, the surviving YB-40s were withdrawn from operational use and used for gunnery training. Their only legacy was the chin gun turret, which had proved an excellent addition to the B-17's armament in action and which was to be incorporated in the last B-17 variant, the B-17G.

THE NAVY'S B-17S

During World War II some 40 B-17Fs were converted to the maritime reconnaissance role, serving with the US Navy as the PB-1, and this maritime task produced an interesting variant. Because of the rudimentary nature of the Japanese air defence system, there was never a priority requirement in the Pacific theatre for electronic intelligence gathering and the development of associated countermeasures systems. However, under a project called Cadillac II, sponsored by the US Government and undertaken by the Massachusetts

Above: After the end of World War II, some B-17s were used as test-beds. This one, bearing the civil registration N5111N, is testing a prototype nose-mounted turboprop engine.

Institute of Technology (MIT), 32 B-17G Flying Fortresses were fitted out as airborne Combat Information Centres (CICs) as a countermeasure against Kamikaze suicide attacks. Designated PB-1W in US Navy service, these aircraft carried an AN/APS 20B search radar in a large belly radome and had a limited fighter direction capability over a range of about 104km (65 miles) against low-flying aircraft and 322km (200 miles) against shipping.

PHOTO RECONNAISSANCE

The first USAAF PR unit to deploy to the European theatre was the 3rd Photo Group under Colonel Elliott Roosevelt, which arrived at Steeple Morden in Cambridgeshire in September 1942 and departed for North Africa two months later. The Group at first used B-17s (F-9s) and Lockheed P-38Es (F-4s), but soon converted to P-38G/Hs, known as F-5As. By the end of 1944 three reconnaissance groups were operational in the Mediterranean theatre, while the Eighth and Ninth Air Forces in England had twenty reconnaissance squadrons at their disposal, equipped with F-5s, F-6s (the PR

Above: A DB-17 Flying Fortress 'Director' used by the 3235th Drone Squadron, Elgin Field, Florida, to control QB-17 drones. Many B-17s ended their days as drones, destroyed in various weapons tests.

version of the P-51 Mustang) and de Havilland Mosquitos Mk XVI, the latter serving with the 25th Bombardment Group at Watton in Norfolk. The 25th BG was formed from the 803rd Squadron, whose countermeasures role under the control of No 100 Group RAF has already been mentioned.

The B-17's reconnaissance role was relatively short-lived, but in the years immediately after World War II it was used extensively by the USAF and US Coast Guard (as the PB-1G) for aerial survey, and some of these missions were of a clandestine nature. In 1946, it was apparent to the Americans that the Russians were probably developing a bomber capable of launching an attack against the continental United States, and that such an attack would have to be made from bases in the Soviet Arctic, the aircraft relying on navigational aids positioned at forward sites in the polar regions, or from the Kamchatka Peninsula in the Far East.

Thanks to a series of well-publicised survey flights made in the 1930s, ostensibly to gather information for setting up a direct long-range air route to the United States, the Russians knew more about the Arctic than anyone else. The

Americans, on the other hand, knew comparatively little, and this gap in their knowledge they were now anxious to fill. In March 1946, therefore, the 46th Reconnaissance Squadron (Very Long Range) was deployed to Ladd Air Force Base in Alaska. Equipped with ten B-29s (including a couple of F-13s fitted out for photoreconnaissance), the 46th RS came under the operational control of the 311th Reconnaissance Wing, which in turn was assigned to the USAF Strategic Air Command, established on 21 March 1946. Following a series of preliminary survey flights over the Arctic by the 46th RS, which mainly involved the checking and upgrading of navigational equipment, the 28th Bombardment Group, a B-29 unit stationed at Grand Island Army Air Field, Nebraska, deployed to Elmendorf in Alaska for a six-month period of training in arctic conditions.

Meanwhile, a detachment of the 311th RW, known as the East Reconnaissance Group, SAC, equipped with F-9 (B-17) photo-mapping aircraft and based at Thule, had begun the aerial mapping of Greenland. This mission was expanded in the following year into Operation Eardrum, with aircraft of the 311th RW surveying the polar area between Iceland and Alaska. So it was that the B-17 Flying Fortress, in a role far removed from its original wartime one, made its own contribution to the Cold War.

Eighth Air Force B-17 Combat Groups, 1942–45

	Base	Code	First Mission	Losses	Comments
34th Bomb Group	Mendelsham		23.5.44	35	Although it had trained on B-17s in the USA, the 34th BG flew Liberators for a time in the ETO before switching back to Fortresses in August 1944. It was the oldest Heavy Bomber Group in the Eighth Air Force, first activated in January 1941. The Group flew some 5500 sorties with its B-17s, dropping 10,160 tonnes (10,000 tons) of bombs. Examples of named B-17s: Rapid City Spook, Dallas Doll, Gotta Haver.
4th Sqn		None			
7th Sqn		None			
18th Sqn		None			
391st Sqn		None			
91st Bomb Group	Bassingbourn		7.11.42	197	First BG to complete 100 missions; total of 340 missions flown (9591 sorties) in which 22,497 tonnes (22,142 tons) of bombs were dropped on enemy targets. Enemy aircraft claimed destroyed: 420. Group nickname: The Ragged Irregulars. Examples of named B-17s: Bad Penny, Memphis Belle, General Ike, Shoo Shoo Shoo Baby, Delta Rebel II.
322nd Sqn		LG			
323rd Sqn		OR			
324th Sqn		DF			
401st Sqn		LL			
92nd Bomb Group	Podington		6.9.42	154	The 92nd BG flew 8633 sorties in 308 missions, dropping 21,164 tonnes (20,830 tons) of bombs and claiming the destruction of 207 enemy aircraft. The Group's 327th Squadron was the only one to use the YB-40 'gunship' variant of the B-17. Examples of named B-17s: Ruthie, Calamity Jane, Pop.
325th Sqn		NV			
326th Sqn		JW			
327th Sqn		UX			
407th Sqn		PY			
94th Bomb Group	Bury St Edmunds		13.5.43	180	The 94th BG flew its first missions from Bassingbourn and Earl's Colne before moving to Bury St Edmunds. The Group flew 8884 sorties in 324 missions, dropping 19,228 tonnes (18,925 tons) of bombs and claiming the destruction of 342 enemy aircraft. Combat losses amounted to 173 out of 180. Examples of named B17s: Ordnance Express, Idiot's delight, House of Lords, Ice Cold Katie, Tutor Wolf, Myazam Dragon.
331st Sqn		ZE			
332nd Sqn		XM			
333rd Sqn		GL			
95th Bomb Group	Horham		13.5.43	196	The 95th BG flew 314 missions, with 8903 individual sorties, and dropped 20,321 tonnes (20,000 tons) of bombs and supplies. Its crews claimed to have destroyed 425 enemy aircraft. Of the group's total losses, 157 were in combat. The 95th took part in the supply operation to the Polish Home Army in Warsaw, September 1944. It was while flying as an observer with the 95th in an attack on Kiel on 13 June 1943 that Brigadier General Nathan B. Forrest was killed, the first American general officer to lose his life in action in the ETO.
334th Sqn		BG			
335th Sqn		OE			
336th Sqn		ET			
412th Sqn		QW			
96th Bomb Group	Snetterton Heath		12.5.43	239	The 96th BG completed 8924 sorties over northwest Europe in 321 missions, dropping 19,812 tonnes (19,500 tons) of bombs. Last combat mission flown on 21 April 1945. The loss figure shown includes 189 in combat. Enemy aircraft claimed destroyed: 354. Examples of named B-17s: The Miracle Tribe, Hang the Expense III, Reluctant Dragon, Paper Doll, The Saint, Sack Time Suzy.
337th Sqn		QJ			
38th Sqn		BX			
339th Sqn		AW			
413th Sqn		MZ			
100th Bomb Group	Thorpe Abbots		22.6.43	229	Nicknamed the 'Bloody Hundredth' because of its severe losses in combat – 177 aircraft out of a total loss of 229 – the 100th BG flew 306 missions, dropping 19,566 tonnes (19,257 tons) of bombs and claiming 261 enemy aircraft destroyed. On 11 October 1943 the 100th BG lost 12 B-17s in an attack on Munster, and 15 in a raid on Berlin on 6 March 1944. It was on this Group that the film 'Twelve o'clock High' was based. Examples of named B-17s: Laden Maiden, Royal Flush, Silver Dollar, Piccadilly Lily.
349th Sqn		XR			
350th Sqn		LN			
351st Sqn		EP			
418th Sqn		LD			
303rd Bomb Group	Molesworth		17.11.42	150	Nicknamed 'Hell's Angels', the 303rd BG became the first Eighth Air Force Group to pass the 300 mission-mark. Two Medals of Honor: Lt Jack W. Mathis received a posthumous award for remaining at his station even though mortally wounded, and T/Sgt Forrest Vosler for remaining at his gun position although seriously wounded in face and thighs. He also managed to fix the B-17's damaged radio by touch. Examples of named B-17s: Hells Angels, Knockout Dropper, The Floose, Wulf Hound, The Winning Run.
358th Sqn		VK			
359th Sqn		BN			
360th Sqn		PU			
427th Sqn		GN			
305th Bomb Group	Chelveston		17.11.42	117	Commanded by Col Curtis E. LeMay, who would later head US Strategic Air Command, the 305th BG completed 337 missions (9231 sorties), dropping 22,724 tonnes (22,365 tons) of bombs and claiming 314 enemy aircraft. Two Medals of Honor: 1st Lt William R. Lawley and 1st Lt Edward S. Mitchell, on 20 February and 11 April 1944 respectively, both for bringing their aircraft home though severely wounded. Examples of named B-17s: Smilin' Thru, Windy City Challenger, Flak Eater, Boom Town, Homesick Angel.
364th Sqn		WF			
365th Sqn		XK			
366th Sqn		KY			
422nd Sqn		JJ			
306th Bomb Group	Thurleigh		9.10.42	171	Between October 1942 and April 1945 the 306th BG flew 342 missions, dropping 22,937 tonnes (22,575 tons) of bombs and claiming 332 enemy aircraft. The Group lost ten B-17s on 17 April 1943 in an attack on Bremen, and another six on 1 May. During this mission Sgt Maynard H. 'Snuffy' Smith, a ball turret gunner, became the only enlisted man in the Eighth Air Force to be awarded the Medal of Honor. Examples of named B-17s: Lassie Come Home, Joan of Arc, Sweet Pea, Satan's Lady, Rose of York.
367th Sqn		GY			
368th Sqn		BO			
369th Sqn		WW			
423rd Sqn		RD			

Base	Code	First Mission	Losses	Comments
351st Bomb Group	Polebrook	12.5.43	124	The 351st BG completed 311 missions, flying 8600 sorties, dropping 20,727 tonnes (20,400 tons) of bombs and leaflets and claiming 303 enemy aircraft. On 20 February 1944 two crew members of the same B-17, 2nd Lt W.E. Truemper and Sgt Archibald Mathies, were awarded posthumous Medals of Honor for taking the controls after the pilot was wounded, allowing the rest of the crew to bale out. They were killed in the ensuing crash. Many of the Group's named B-17s had 'Ball' in their name, eg: Spitball, Speedball, Screwball, Fireball, Cannon Ball and (predictably) No Balls at All.
508th Sqn	YB			
509th Sqn	RQ			
510th Sqn	TU			
511th Sqn	DS			
379th Bomb Group	Kimbolton	31.5.43	141	In the course of 330 missions the 379th BG flew a total of 10,492 sorties, more than any other in the Eighth Air Force, dropping 26,925 tonnes (26,500 tons) of bombs and leaflets and claiming the destruction of 249 enemy aircraft. Examples of named B-17s: Dangerous Dan, Birmingham Jewel, The Lost Angel, Duffy's Tavern.
524th Sqn	WA			
525th Sqn	FR			
526th Sqn	LF			
527th Sqn	FO			
381st Bomb Group	Ridgewell	22.6.44	131	The 381st BG flew over 9000 sorties over Europe, dropping 21,489 tonnes (21,150 tons) of bombs. Enemy aircraft claimed destroyed: 223. Last mission flown on 25 April 1945. Examples of named B-17s: Phyliss, RAFAAF, Stage Door Canteen, Tinkertoy, Yardbird II, Linda Mary.
532nd Sqn	VE			
533rd Sqn	VP			
534th Sqn	GD			
535th Sqn	MS			
384th Bomb Group	Grafton Underwood	22.6.43	159	The 384th BG flew 316 missions, totalling 9348 sorties, and dropped 22,775 tonnes (22,415 tons) of bombs. Its crews claimed the destruction of 165 enemy aircraft. On 25 April 1945, the Group dropped the last American bombs of WWII on a target in Europe. Examples of named B-17s: The Joker, Green Mountain Gal, Royal Flush, Vertical Shaft, Tremblin Gremlin.
544th Sqn	SU			
545th Sqn	JD			
546th Sqn	BK			
547th Sqn	SO			
385th Bomb Group	Great Ashfield	17.7.43	169	The 385th BG flew 8264 sorties in the course of 296 combat missions, dropping 18,797 tonnes (18,500 tons) of bombs and claiming 287 enemy aircraft. On 19 February 1945, one of its aircraft, Satan's Mate (Lt Jim Fleiser) inadvertently looped as it hit another aircraft's slipstream; it reached a speed of 611km/h (380mph) before the pilot recovered, suffering only a few popped rivets. Examples of named B-17s: Ohio Air Force, Pregnant Portia, Powerful Katrina, Dragon Lady, Lulu Belle, Piccadilly Queen.
548th Sqn	None			
549th Sqn	None			
550th Sqn	None			
551st Sqn	None			
388th Bomb Group	Knettishall	17.7.43	202	The 388th BG flew a total of 8051 combat sorties in 306 missions, dropping 18,898 tonnes (18,600 tons) of bombs. Of its losses, 162 were in action, including 14 at Poltava, USSR. The 388th lost 524 men killed in action, 48 interned, 43 missing and 742 PoW. Examples of named B-17s: Old Ironsides, Pistol Packin' Mama, Battlin' Betty, Iza Angel II, Cutie on Duty, Ole Basser, Shoo Shoo Baby, Wolf Pack, Tom Paine, Ramp Tramp, Blitzin' Betsy, Jamaica Ginger, Classy Chassey, In God We Trust, Thunderbird.
560th Sqn	None			
561st Sqn	None			
562nd Sqn	None			
563rd Sqn	None			
390th Bomb Group	Framlingham	12.8.43	176	The 390th BG flew 300 missions, dropping over 19,305 tonnes (19,000 tons) of bombs, and claimed to have destroyed 343 enemy aircraft. Of the losses stated above, 144 were in combat. The Group lost six aircraft on the Schweinfurt mission, 14 October 1943, and eight on a mission to Munster on 9 October 1944. Examples of named B-17s: Spot Remover, Royal Flush, Bad Penny, Blood Guts and Rust, Six Nights in Telegma, I'll Get By, Stork Club.
568th Sqn	BI			
569th Sqn	CC			
570th Sqn	DI			
571st Sqn	FC			
398th Bomb Group	Nuthampstead	6.5.44	58	The 398th BG flew 195 missions (6419 sorties), dropping 16,033 tonnes (15,780 tons) of bombs. The Group's 601st Sqn lost six B-17s on 13 April 1945, destroyed by the premature release of two RDX bombs which exploded under a formation. Enemy aircraft claimed destroyed: five. Examples of named B-17s: Old Blood-N-Guts, Nutty Hussy.
600th Sqn	N8			
601st Sqn	30			
602nd Sqn	K8			
603rd Sqn	N7			
401st Bomb Group	Deenethorpe	26.11.43	95	The 401st BG completed 255 combat missions, flying 7430 individual sorties, dropping 18,080 tonnes (17,795 tons) of bombs and claiming the destruction of 75 enemy aircraft. Examples of named B-17s: Fancy Nancy, Battlin' Betty, Nasty Habit, Der Grossarshvogel, Back Buster, Miss B. Haven, Mary Alice.
612th Sqn	SC			
613th Sqn	IN			
614th Sqn	IW			
615th Sqn	IY			
447th Bomb Group	Rattlesden	24.12.43	153	During its combat career the 447th BG flew 7605 sorties, dropping 17,273 tonnes (17,000 tons) of bombs and also 401 tonnes (395 tons) of supplies to the French Forces of the Interior. The Group claimed 342 enemy aircraft. One of the Group's navigators, 2nd Lt Robert E. Femoyer, was awarded a posthumous Medal of Honor for remaining at his post, despite severe wounds, to guide his aircraft clear of heavy flak on its homeward flight. He died shortly after being taken to hospital. Examples of named B-17s: Milk Wagon (129 missions), A Bit of Lace, El Lobo, American Beauty, Bugs Bunny Jr., Feather Merchant, Vat 69.
708th Sqn	CO			
709th Sqn	IE			
710th Sqn	IF			
711th Sqn	IR			
452nd Bomb Group	Deopham Green	16.2.44	158	The 452nd BG flew 250 missions totalling 7279 individual sorties, dropping 16,721 tonnes (16,457 tons) of bombs and claiming 96.5 enemy aircraft. On 9 November 1944, during an attack on Metz and Thionville, two of the Group's personnel, Lts Donald J. Gott and William E. Metzger, Jr (pilot and co-pilot) attempted to land their burning B-17 in a forest clearing in order to save their badly injured radioman, but the aircraft exploded, killing all three. Gott and Metzger were awarded posthumous Medals of Honor. Examples of named B-17s: Dinah Mite, Big Time Operator, Big Noise, Lady Satan, E-Rat-Icator.
728th Sqn	9Z			
729th Sqn	M3			
730th Sqn	6K			
731st Sqn	7D			

	Base	Code	First Mission	Losses	Comments
Bomb Group	Glatton		21.2.44	83	Known as the Fireball Outfit, the 457th BG was the first Group to dispense with camouflage and put up an all natural metal formation. It completed 236 missions, totalling 7086 sorties, dropped some 17,272 tonnes (17,000 tons) of bombs and claimed the destruction of 33 enemy aircraft. Examples of named B-17s: Paper War, Miss Cue, Flak Dodger, El Lobo II.
748th Sqn		None			
749th Sqn		None			
750th Sqn		None			
751st Sqn		None			
486th Bomb Group	Sudbury		7.5.44	21	Originally equipped with B-24 Liberators, the 486th BG received B-17Gs in July 1944 and flew 142 missions (4629 sorties) in Fortresses, dropping 11,063 tonnes (10,888 tons) of bombs. The Group claimed the destruction of 17 enemy aircraft destroyed. In the closing months of the war the 486th was extensively employed in support of Allied ground forces advancing through northwest Europe. Examples of named B-17s: Rack and Run, Lush Through.
832nd Sqn		3R			
833rd Sqn		4N			
834th Sqn		2S			
835th Sqn		H8			
487th Bomb Group	Lavenham		7.5.44	26	The 487th BG flew some 4600 combat sorties during its year of operations, dropping 10,668 tonnes (10,500 tons) of bombs. A posthumous Medal of Honor was awarded to Brigadier General Frank Castle, commanding the 3rd Air Division, for attempting to crash-land a badly damaged 487th BG Fortress near Liége, Belgium, in order to save two wounded crew members on 24 December 1944. Examples of named B-17s: High Tailed Lady, Banshee, Gravel Gerties Crew.
836th Sqn		2G			
837th Sqn		4F			
838th Sqn		2C			
839th Sqn		R5			
490th Bomb Group	Eye		31.5.44	27	The 490th BG flew 40 missions with B-24 Liberators before converting to B-17Gs on 24 August 1944. In addition to attacking strategic targets, the Group flew many tactical sorties, especially during the Ardennes offensive in December 1944. After the end of hostilities it dropped supplies into Holland and transported PoWs. It left Eye in August 1945.
848th Sqn		None			
849th Sqn		None			
850th Sqn		None			
851st Sqn		None			
493rd Bomb Group	Debach		8.9.44	32	Like the 490th BG, the 493rd flew B-24s before switching to B-17s, with which it completed 110 missions. Seven of its combat losses were sustained in one attack on Magdeburg.
860th Sqn		None			
861st Sqn		None			
862nd Sqn		None			
863rd Sqn		None			

The B-17 Compared with other Heavy Bombers

	BOEING B-17F FORTRESS	CONSOLIDATED B-24J LIBERATOR	AVRO LANCASTER B1	HANDLEY PAGE HALIFAX BIII	HEINKEL He 177 GREIF
Engines:	Four 1200hp Wright R-1820-97 Cyclone radials	Four 1200hp Pratt & Whitney R-1830-65 Twin Wasp radials	Four 1280hp Rolls-Royce Merlin inline engines	Four 1615hp Bristol Hercules XVI radials	Four 2950 Daimler-Benz DB610 radial engines (coupled pairs)
Span:	31.6m (103ft 9in)	33.53m (110ft)	31.09m (102ft)	31.75m (104ft 2in)	31.44m (103ft 2in)
Length:	22.7m (74ft 8in)	20.47m (67ft 2in)	21.13m (69ft 4in)	21.82m (71ft 7in)	22m (72ft 2in)
Height:	5.8m (19ft 2in)	5.37m (17ft 7in)	5.97m (19ft 7in)	6.32m (20ft 9in)	6.4m (21ft)
Normal T/O Weight:	24,948kg (55,000lb)	25,401kg (56,000lb)	29,898kg (66,000lb)	24,675kg (54,400lb)	27,200kg (59,966lb)
Max Speed:	504km/h (313mph) at 7620m (25,000ft)	467km/h (290 mph) at 7620m (25,000ft)	462km/hr (287mph) at 3505m (11,500ft)	454km/h (282mph) at 4115m (13,500ft)	488km/h (303mph) at 6100m (20,010ft)
Ceiling:	1,431m (37,500ft)	8534m (28,000ft)	7467m (24,500ft)	7315m (24,000ft)	8082m (26,500ft)
Range:	2092km (1300 miles) with 2722kg (6000lb) bomb load	3380km (2100 miles) with 2268kg (5000lb) bomb load	2784km (1730 miles) with 5443kg (12,000lb) bomb load	1658km (1030 miles) with 5897kg (13,000lb) of bombs	5000km (3107 miles) with two Henschel Hs293 missiles
Armament:	Eight or nine 0.50in Browning machine guns	Ten 0.50in Browning machine guns	Eight 0.303 machine guns	Eight 0.303in Browning and one 0.303in Vickers K guns	Two 20mm cannon, three 13mm MG131 and three 7.9mm MG
Max Bomb Load:	5806kg (12,800lb)	5436kg (12,800lb)	8154kg (18,000lb)	5897kg (13,000lb)	1000kg (2205lb)
Crew:	10	12	7	7	6

INDEX